CONCISE
LINCOLN
LIBRARY

—

EDITED BY RICHARD W. ETULAIN,
SARA VAUGHN GABBARD, AND
SYLVIA FRANK RODRIGUE

JOHN DAVID SMITH

Lincoln and the U.S. Colored Troops

Southern Illinois University Press
Carbondale

16 15 14 13   4 3 2 1

The Concise Lincoln Library has been made possible in part
through a generous donation by the Leland E. and LaRita
R. Boren Trust.

Publication of this book has been partially supported by a
subvention from the College of Liberal Arts and Sciences,
University of North Carolina at Charlotte.

Library of Congress Cataloging-in-Publication Data
Smith, John David, 1949–
Lincoln and the U.S. Colored Troops / John David Smith.
    pages cm. — (Concise Lincoln library)
Includes bibliographical references and index.
ISBN 978-0-8093-3290-8 (cloth : alk. paper)
ISBN 0-8093-3290-6 (cloth : alk. paper)
ISBN 978-0-8093-3291-5 (ebook)
ISBN 0-8093-3291-4 (ebook)
1. United States—History—Civil War, 1861–1865—
Participation, African American. 2. United States. Colored
Troops. 3. Lincoln, Abraham, 1809–1865—Relations with
African Americans. 4. United States. Army—African
American troops—History—19th century. 5. African
American soldiers—History—19th century. I. Title.
E540.N3S67 2013
973.7'415—dc23   2013011435

Printed on recycled paper. ♻
The paper used in this publication meets the mini-
mum requirements of American National Standard
for Information Sciences—Petrmanence of Paper for
Printed Library Materials, ANSI Z39.48-1992. ∞

Für Max—der meinem Leben viel Freude gebracht hat

CONTENTS

LINCOLN AND THE U.S. COLORED TROOPS

INTRODUCTION

On March 30, 1864, Private Hannibal Cox, an infantryman in the Fourteenth U.S. Colored Troops (USCT), sent President Abraham Lincoln a gift—a poem that he had written at his military post in Chattanooga, Tennessee. Cox described himself as "a Man of no Education" who had "been Doomed to Slavery." He was born in Powhatan County, Virginia, raised in Richmond, and eventually became the property of a slaveholder named Green in Lincoln County, Tennessee. In August 1863, Cox escaped to the U.S. General Hospital at Tullahoma, Tennessee, where Dr. Benjamin Woodward, surgeon of the Twenty-Second Illinois Volunteer Infantry, took him in. Soldiers taught Cox how to read and write, and in spring 1864 he enlisted in the Fourteenth USCT.[1]

Cox informed Lincoln that although he had left his wife and children to join the army, "I have not yet for Saken them." He decided to make "one grasp at the Flag of the union and Declared it shall never fall." Cox hoped that he would meet Lincoln "in the bonds of love" and bid him "fare well," hopeful that "History may tell." In a postscript Cox added: "I. sends this for you to look at you must not laugh at it."[2]

Dr. Woodward, who had heard Lincoln speak in Springfield before he left for Washington in 1861, described Cox, the escaped slave and soldier, as "but a sample of the glorious fruits of Your 'Proclamation' of Liberty.'" Woodward reminded the president that as he departed for his inaugural, he admonished the audience to

"Pray for me." Now, the surgeon explained, "a thousand hearts responded, and we . . . thank God who has so 'led You into all truth' and thousands in the army rejoice in Your work and pray for you that you may be sustained till the great work which God has called You to is fully accomplished."[3]

Lincoln left no record of his impressions of Cox's poem. But it is doubtful that he laughed at it. By war's end, the army had raised 178,975 enlisted men for the USCT. The War Department's Bureau of Colored Troops organized the soldiers in 133 infantry regiments, four independent companies, seven cavalry regiments, twelve regiments of heavy artillery, and ten batteries of light artillery. Roughly 19 percent of the troops came from the eighteen northern states, 24 percent from the four Union slave states, and 57 percent from the eleven Confederate states. The 1860 Federal census reported around 750,000 male slaves, most residing in the Rebel states, of arms-bearing age and, accordingly, the majority of the men of the USCT were ex-slaves. Not only did slaves recruited in the South bolster Union armies, but they also denied the Rebels a sizable workforce, around eighty thousand bonded laborers. Overall 21 percent of the nation's adult male black population between ages eighteen and forty-five joined the USCT, including almost three-quarters of all men in the free states of military age. Altogether, African Americans accounted for between 9 and 12 percent of all Union troops who served in the war. The USCT signified the first systematic, large-scale effort by the U.S. government to arm African Americans to aid in the nation's defense.[4]

Just as the men of the USCT associated their freedom and military service with Lincoln and his administration, the president had become deeply appreciative of the African American soldiers' contributions to the hard-fought Union victory.[5] Lincoln experienced a metamorphosis during the war, which by mid-1862 had become a stalemate between the forces of slavery and southern independence on the one hand, and those of free labor and national Union on the other. For months he had marked time making only "small, token gestures" toward freeing the slaves.[6] Finally on January 1, 1863, Lincoln issued the final Emancipation Proclamation, a military decree that freed and armed the Rebels' slaves.

Eight months later, after black troops had distinguished themselves in bloody combat at Fort Wagner near Charleston, South Carolina, Lincoln informed a friend that his field commanders, including those unsympathetic to abolitionism, now believed that "the emancipation policy, and the use of colored troops, constitute the heaviest blow yet dealt to the rebellion; and that, at least one of those important successes, could not have been achieved when it was, but for the aid of black soldiers." The president predicted that African Americans would "remember that, with silent tongue, and clenched teeth, and steady eye, and well-poised bayonet, they have helped mankind on to this great consummation." He also anticipated that some future white people, referring to northern Copperheads, "unable to forget that, with malignant heart, and deceitful speech, they have strove to hinder it."[7]

Early in the war, however, Lincoln had publicly opposed emancipation and the military mobilization of black men, convinced that Congress lacked authority to eliminate slavery as a state institution. Then he favored gradual emancipation with compensation and repatriation of slaves belonging to loyal slaveholders. Finally he concluded that to defeat the Rebels and restore the Union required freeing the slaves under the president's war powers. He did so incrementally by military force, mobilizing the Confederacy's slaves and northern free black men as soldiers. In the sweep of two years Lincoln switched from opposing the arming of African Americans to championing it enthusiastically. Lincoln's emancipation edict was unquestionably a revolutionary military move.[8] Its provision to arm America's black men revolutionized America and empowered its African American population. Years later the Reverend Henry McNeal Turner, who served as chaplain of the First USCT, described January 1, 1863, as "indeed a time of times, and a half time, nothing like it will ever be seen again in this life."[9]

Immediate emancipation constituted a radical departure from the norm; heretofore when slave societies throughout the world liberated their bondsmen and women, they did so gradually, as some form of gradual apprenticeship.[10] After 1863 gradual emancipation no longer appeared in Lincoln's lexicon and he abandoned plans to colonize people of color beyond America's borders. During Lincoln's personal evolution to freeing and arming the slaves, he slowly came to understand the determination of black people to convert the war for the Union into a war for African American freedom.

"The slaves certainly had no doubts about the power of the Proclamation," writes historian Allen C. Guelzo. "It was from the Proclamation that blacks over and over again dated a conclusive sense of liberation from slavery, even if in practice they remained slaves."[11] In early January 1863, for example, Colonel Thomas W. Higginson was leading the First South Carolina Volunteers, the first regiment of former slaves formally authorized by the War Department, on a raid up the St. Marys River along the Florida-Georgia border. Massachusetts governor John A. Andrew had supplied Higginson with printed copies of the newly issued Emancipation Proclamation, which the colonel issued to his men to carry with them. Though many of the black soldiers were illiterate and could not read Lincoln's proclamation, as Higginson later explained in his *Army Life in a Black Regiment* (1869), they nonetheless "all seemed to feel more secure when they held it in their hands."[12]

Black soldiers ultimately helped to fashion both Union victory and the war's meaning. More so than any other step Lincoln took toward suppressing the slaveholders' rebellion, African American military service positioned the question of black citizenship at center stage. Once armed, black men instantly assumed a new status, entering one of America's oldest and most honored institutions—the U.S. Army. Their integration—figuratively, *not* literally—into the American military and the black soldiers' solid record in fighting the Confederates proved crucial in defeating the insurgents. Their service also raised numerous vexing questions about their postwar legal status—questions that Lincoln had only begun to think about when General Robert E. Lee surrendered at Appomattox.[13]

In mid-1863, the president explained to the ex-slave and black abolitionist Frederick Douglass, who had goaded the president to free and arm the slaves since 1861, that the heroism displayed by the men of the USCT in its first battles—at Fort Wagner outside of Charleston, at Milliken's Bend and Port Hudson, Louisiana—constituted necessary "preparatory work" for him to make the case for limited black suffrage for black males.[14] He made much the same point in March 1864, hinting to Michael Hahn, Louisiana's military governor, that some "colored people," including "the very intelligent, and especially those who have fought gallantly in our ranks," might be enfranchised in Louisiana's new state constitution. With much prescience, Lincoln wrote: "They would probably help in some trying time to come, to keep the jewel of liberty within the family of freedom."[15] And in what became Lincoln's final public address, on April 11, 1865, the president intimated that the electoral franchise in Louisiana, and implicitly also in other soon-to-be-reconstructed southern states, might be "conferred on the very intelligent [African American men], and on those who serve our cause as soldiers."[16] By the time of his death Lincoln had concluded that because of their contributions to sustaining the Union, enfranchising the men of the USCT was a moral obligation.[17] Three days after Lincoln hinted that the franchise might be awarded to men, who served in the USCT, John Wilkes Booth struck him down.

When pressed to defend emancipation, Lincoln commonly resorted to pragmatic arguments, but by mid-1862 he concluded that emancipation "was both morally right and also expedient as a means of prosecuting the war against the Southern Confederacy."[18] Late in the war he explained in an interview the contributions of the USCT. In terms of manpower, Lincoln said, black men added around two hundred thousand men to the Union cause, concomitantly denying that number to the Confederates. They defended important military posts along the Union's offensive line. If Lincoln abandoned those posts, he said, the war would be lost in three weeks. He and the country needed what Lincoln referred to as "the black warriors of Port Hudson & Olustee." The president made clear that the cause of restoring the Union and abolishing slavery were one and the same. Employing one of his favorite metaphors, Lincoln stated: "no human power can subdue this rebellion without using the Emancipation lever as I have done." "My enemies condemn my emancipation policy. Let them prove by the history of this war, that we can restore the Union without it."[19]

Some consider the president's emancipation project part of a policy of "total war." Unquestionably, Lincoln's evolving program of confiscation then emancipation then military mobilization of black men gave the Confederates a clear message, as he informed Maryland Democrat Reverdy Johnson "that I shall not surrender this game leaving any available card unplayed."[20] London's illustrated magazine *Punch* borrowed Lincoln's metaphor. In October 1862 it published a cartoon of Lincoln and Confederate president Jefferson Davis playing cards on a makeshift table atop a keg of gunpowder. In the cartoon Lincoln raises his trump card—a black soldier.[21]

A year earlier, Lincoln had begun his two-part military emancipation program. Phase one culminated on New Year's Day 1863 with the president's final Emancipation Proclamation, freeing persons of color enslaved in Confederate-held territory and authorizing the mobilization of black men as armed soldiers. As commander in chief, he welcomed African Americans "into the armed service of the United States to garrison forts, positions, stations, and other places, and to man vessels of all sorts in said service."[22] Part two resulted as slaves from across the Confederacy and the border states freed themselves, entered Union lines, and joined Federal forces not as laborers, but as armed soldiers. In the USCT they overcame all manner of white racism, overt and covert, as well as war crimes by Confederates, to prove their worth as men.

Extirpating slavery in the Confederacy and then arming free black men and freedmen were landmark steps in Lincoln's transformative emancipation project. The president recalled that he decided to arm the black men out of "a clear conviction of duty . . . to turn that element of strength to account," and for that decision he alone was responsible "to the American people, to the christian world, to history, and on my final account to God."[23] Many white northerners, however, considered Lincoln's emancipation program controversial and radical, at best experimental.[24] Fearing racial conflict, and determined to keep black troops at bay, white Philadelphians positioned Camp William Penn, the largest USCT recruitment center in the North, eight miles out of town.[25] White southerners, not surprisingly, worried that armed black soldiers would unleash racial chaos in their slave society.

Unquestionably, emancipation exacerbated white southerners' worst fears of race war and servile insurrection. To suppress their rebellion Lincoln had transformed the conflict from a constitutional struggle to restore the Union to "a social revolution of unprecedented scale."[26]

During the last two years of the war, the men of the USCT fought in combat divisions in the Armies of the Cumberland, the James, and the Potomac. Admittedly, most of the black troops participated primarily in minor engagements, not in major campaigns. Nonetheless, the men of the USCT fought in 449 separate engagements. They served in every military theater, in the East, the West, in the Mississippi Valley, and in the Trans-Mississippi. They entered combat as early as October 29, 1862 (a skirmish at Island Mound, Missouri, by the First Kansas Colored Volunteers), and continued fighting until May 11–12, 1865 (skirmishes at Palmito Ranch, Texas, involving the Sixty-Second USCT), a month after Lee surrendered. Sixteen black enlisted men received the Medal of Honor, awarded for the first time in 1863.[27]

Arming the South's newly freed slaves and free black men from the North had sweeping implications both for them and the nation. Not only did emancipation provide much-needed manpower for the Union army, it converted the Union military effort into a moral crusade, a war of African American liberation with lasting consequences for all Americans. For the first time in American history, people of color established a direct relationship with the U.S. government—no longer as chattel property protected only by state laws. Their wartime struggles to obtain equal treatment from the army, and from white Americans generally, prepared the men of the USCT to demand national citizenship rights—and true equality—during Reconstruction and for a century afterward.[28]

The one hundred days between Lincoln's issuing the preliminary and final versions of the Emancipation Proclamation constitute one of the most compelling and important stories in American history.[29] Lincoln's role in the arming of African Americans remains a central but unfortunately undertold part of this saga.

After January 1863 the president's moves to free the Confederates' slaves, and then to recruit and deploy black soldiers, occupied a key place in Union military policy. They are the subjects of this book.

THE FINAL EMANCIPATION
PROCLAMATION AND
MILITARY EMANCIPATION

On January 1, 1863, Abraham Lincoln declared "as a fit and necessary war measure" that slaves held in Confederate territory "henceforward shall be free." After imploring the newly freed slaves to "abstain from all violence, unless in necessary self-defence," the president proclaimed "that such persons of suitable condition, will be received into the armed service of the United States to garrison forts, positions, stations, and other places, and to man vessels of all sorts in said service."[1] A month later, three thousand men and women assembled at a meeting in Brooklyn, New York, and gave the president's military emancipation project a ringing endorsement: "Where ever you see a black man—give him a Gun & tell him to aid in saving the Republic."[2] For all its heady promise in early 1863, however, Lincoln had taken twenty-one months to settle on a policy of military emancipation. Unable to suppress the Confederate insurgents by conventional military means, and after months of prodding politicians to accept various gradual emancipation and compensated emancipation schemes, Lincoln settled on general emancipation as the final weapon with which to crush the slaveholders' rebellion.

To be sure, Lincoln moved prudently, hopeful to keep the Union intact with slavery. When summoning the militia to suppress the rebellion in April 1861, he assured white southerners that "the utmost care will be observed . . . to avoid any devastation, any destruction of, or interference with, property, or any disturbance of peaceful citizens in any part of the country." And when, in May 1861, Frederick Douglass clamored for "*carrying the war into Africa.' Let the slaves and free colored people be called into service, and formed into a liberating army*," Lincoln demurred. Like most white northerners, early in the war he defined the conflict, according to the Reverend John G. Fee, a radical abolitionist from Berea, Kentucky, as a "white man's war," committed to "let the nigger stay where he is."[3]

While African Americans had fought in the American Revolution and the War of 1812, a point that proponents of utilizing black soldiers emphasized repeatedly, since 1792 Federal law prohibited black men from serving in the state militias and the U.S. Army. Outraged by discussions of arming the South's slaves, late in 1861 the *New York Express* predicted that should "this be attempted to any extent, the whole world will cry out against our inhumanity, our savagery, and the sympathies of all mankind will be turned against us." This attitude was common among both northern white civilians and soldiers in the Union army until 1863, when regiments of black troops filled depleted Union armies and proved their fighting ability in combat.[4]

Lincoln understood the implications for social change that emancipation and the use of black men as soldiers implied. These steps, including the possibility of placing black people on a social and political par with white people, would challenge the nation's racial status quo—white supremacy. They would fuel the racial phobias of conservative Democrats and Republicans and would discourage white enlistments. Lincoln also worried that emancipation would alienate slaveholders and non-slaveholders alike in the loyal border states and might further work to unify opposition to the Union in the Confederate states. These were legitimate fears. Americans tended to identify bearing arms and citizenship.[5]

Once white southerners engaged in armed rebellion, however, Lincoln systematically reneged on his promise not to interfere with slaveholders' private property. To some degree he was forced to do so. The Confederacy's early military successes depended significantly on slavery. Bondsmen provided the agricultural and industrial labor that supplied its armies. Slaves constructed fortifications, repaired railroads, and freed up white men to serve in the ranks. In response, Lincoln began a series of deliberate steps that culminated in his emancipating and arming African Americans. In his private and public pronouncements the president used the idea of contingency as a rhetorical device to make his emancipation project palatable to a broad community of white northerners. Ultimately he could not suppress the rebellion without using his "Emancipation lever."

* * *

Lincoln launched his emancipation project very early in the war. He proffered no objections when in May 1861 General Benjamin F. Butler, commanding Union troops at Fortress Monroe, Virginia, unilaterally refused to return fugitive slaves employed by the Confederates, declaring them "contraband of war." As soon as the war began, slaves flooded Federal lines in the border South, emancipating themselves, and continued to inundate army camps as Federal armies enveloped the Confederacy. Butler declined to render the runaway bondsmen to their Rebel masters; instead he put them to work in his quartermaster department. Butler reasoned that surrendering the slaves to their owners would aid the enemy; employing them as laborers would help the Union. With no established policy of his own on the slavery question, but leaning in the direction of emancipation, Lincoln let Butler's ad hoc policy stand.[6]

Underestimating the slaves' desire to be free and to contribute to their own emancipation, and ever mindful of losing border state and northern conservative support, from the fall 1861 to the spring 1862 Lincoln instructed his commanders officially to exclude runaway slaves from Federal lines. But the bondsmen kept coming, gradually convincing soldiers, their officers, politicians, northern public opinion, and finally Lincoln of their importance as a strategic weapon against the Rebels. Following Butler's lead, the army employed them as military laborers. "It is a military necessary," the president explained in July 1862, "to have men and money; and we can get neither, in sufficient numbers, or amounts, if we keep from, or drive from, our lines, slaves coming to them."[7]

The slaves themselves made the clearest case for emancipation. "In time," Ira Berlin explains, "it became evident even to the most obtuse Federal commanders that every slave who crossed into Union lines was a double gain: one subtracted from the Confederacy and one added to the Union." As "contrabands" hundreds of thousands of fugitive slaves worked as teamsters, blacksmiths, cooks, coopers, carpenters, bakers, butchers, laundresses, personal servants, and performed other menial duties. While the slaves may or may not have "forced the issue" of emancipation on the president, they ultimately depended on Lincoln to free and arm them.[8]

On August 6, 1861, Congress passed the First Confiscation Act, authorizing the government to seize all property, including slaves, used by Confederates "to work or to be employed in or upon any fort, navy yard, dock, armory, ship, entrenchment, or in any military or naval service whatsoever, against the Government and lawful authority of the United States." Over the course of the war, more than two hundred thousand contrabands worked for the U.S. Army as cattle drivers, stevedores, and pioneer laborers, and in other support roles. Though Butler's "contraband of war" policy and the First Confiscation Act sidestepped the question of manumission, they nevertheless introduced "the thin edge of the wedge of emancipation" into Federal military policy.[9] Lincoln considered the confiscation bill ill-timed and premature. He feared that it might encourage border state slaveholders to join the Rebels.[10]

General John C. Frémont's August 30, 1861, proclamation unilaterally freeing the slaves of Missouri Rebels worried Lincoln even more. Frémont assumed erroneously that the First Confiscation Act empowered him to emancipate slaves within the Department of the West. Annoyed that the general had usurped congressional imperatives, and fearful that emancipation would drive Kentucky into the Confederacy, the president rescinded Frémont's edict on September 11. "I think to lose Kentucky is nearly the same as to lose the whole game," Lincoln informed his friend Senator Orville H. Browning. "Kentucky gone, we can not hold Missouri, nor, as I think, Maryland. These all against us, and the job on our hands is too large for us." Outraged by Lincoln's revocation of Frémont's order, radical abolitionist Parker Pillsbury condemned the president's "cowardly submission to Southern and border slave state dictation."[11]

Though Lincoln's reprimand of Frémont gave the impression that he opposed military emancipation, early in the war actions by War Department officials and military officers in the field gave another. In October 1861, as General Thomas W. Sherman began an expedition to South Carolina's coastal islands, acting Secretary of War Thomas A. Scott instructed him obliquely to "avail yourself of the services of any persons, whether fugitives from labor or not." Ostensibly referring to Confederate slaves or fugitive slaves, Scott authorized Sherman to organize and employ them as he wished, but Scott made clear his order did not constitute "a general arming of them for military service."[12] Though Sherman failed to use the black men for military purposes, in December 1861 Scott's superior, Secretary of War Simon Cameron, incorporated a call for the enlistment of black soldiers into his annual report, another unilateral move that Lincoln squelched.[13]

The Frémont and Cameron matters displeased Lincoln. In a letter to a Kentucky editor, the president, concerned that their actions might jeopardize border state and northern conservative support, explained his side of the story: "When, early in the war, Gen. Frémont attempted military emancipation, I forbade it, because I did not think it an indispensable necessity. When a little later, Gen. Cameron, then Secretary of War, suggested the arming of the blacks, I objected, because I did not yet think it an indispensable necessity." Influential "advanced" Republicans, abolitionist politicians who advocated complete black equality, including Pennsylvania congressman Thaddeus Stevens and Massachusetts senator Charles Sumner, sided with Cameron. In December 1861, Illinois congressman Owen Lovejoy proclaimed that it would be impossible to defeat the southern states "without liberating their slaves and putting muskets into the hands of all who will fight for us." A critic of Lincoln's from St. Louis agreed, charging that by rebuking Cameron, the president "has given another evidence of that weak vacillation which has characterized all his actions in this war." The editor of the *Chicago Tribune* sent a message to Cameron: "You were right and he [Lincoln] was wrong."[14]

Variants of the Frémont case occurred again in May 1862, when Federal officers in different military theatres enlisted black men without War Department authorization. In Kansas, General James ("Jim") H. Lane, a former U.S. senator, recruited fugitive slaves along with Native Americans from Arkansas and Missouri. Though twice denied permission to do so, the irrepressible Lane nevertheless continued to enlist what became the First Kansas Colored Volunteers, the first black regiment recruited in a northern state.[15]

In Federal-occupied Louisiana, General John W. Phelps requested permission from his superior, General Benjamin F. Butler, then commanding the Department of the Gulf, to recruit fugitive slaves at Camp Parapet near New Orleans. Beginning in May 1862, Phelps made Camp Parapet a refuge for runaway slaves and instructed his men to retaliate against slaveholders who had mistreated their bondsmen. Deeply committed to emancipation and black enlistment as means to weaken the Confederacy and to incite the slaves against their former masters, Phelps implored Butler to allow him to arm the slaves in his camp. Butler refused, arguing that he lacked authorization from Lincoln to enlist black soldiers and also doubting the necessity and quality of African American troops. Like Lane, Phelps was a radical abolitionist who believed that regarding emancipation and the enlistment of black troops at least, he was answerable to a "higher law" than Lincoln. Without authority, in July 1862, Phelps raised five companies of black troops with hopes of arming them. Instead of supplying Phelps's men with guns, however, Butler issued them saws. He ordered the men to cut trees around camp, not drill.[16]

Outraged, Phelps refused to obey Butler's order and resigned his commission. In August 1862, Butler, then desperate for reinforcements, reversed course and decided "to call on Africa," accepting the Louisiana Native Guards, a regiment of elite New Orleans free black militiamen that previously had offered its services to the Confederates, as volunteers. By November Butler had mustered three regiments of Louisiana Native Guards (Union), including their black officers, into Federal service, making him the first Union commander to bring free blacks formally into the Union ranks. For the remainder of the war Butler championed the use of African American troops.

He was one of the few high ranking generals who refused to consider black soldiers little more than "uniformed ditchdiggers." Near the end of the war Butler commanded the Army of the James and its Twenty-Fifth Corps, the first and only army corps in American history composed entirely of African Americans.[17]

While the recruitment efforts of Lane and Phelps in distant Kansas and Louisiana, respectively, attracted little national attention, those of Lincoln's friend, General David Hunter, commander of the Department of the South, grabbed national headlines. On May 9, 1862, Hunter unilaterally declared martial law and liberated bondsmen around Fort Pulaski, Georgia, determined to put them to work as laborers. Hunter professed to assume erroneously that he possessed the same authorization from the War Department accorded Sherman to mobilize slave soldiers. Lacking War Department authorization, however, Hunter nevertheless proclaimed slaves in sections of coastal South Carolina, Georgia, and Florida free and ordered the enlistment as soldiers of all physically fit black men between the ages of eighteen and forty-five.[18] A week following Hunter's proclamation, Carl Schurz, the influential German American Republican and Union general, advised Lincoln to respond to Hunter's decree carefully. He explained to Lincoln that emancipation was inevitable and could be rationalized as resulting from "local military necessity." Ignoring Schurz's advice, Lincoln annulled Hunter's emancipation decree on May 19 but, significantly, remained silent about the general's military recruiting.[19]

Lincoln overruled Hunter, unconvinced that emancipating African Americans was yet a "necessity." Significantly, in revoking Hunter's proclamation, Lincoln made clear that no military commander had the constitutional authority to free and arm slaves; only the president held those powers.[20] Lincoln could not allow the overly zealous Hunter to proceed with his emancipation plan at the very moment that he was developing his own program of gradual and compensated emancipation and colonization for the border slave states.[21] So, without fanfare, and probably as a test case (as with Lane in Kansas), Lincoln repudiated Hunter's emancipation decree but silently allowed him to recruit blacks in South Carolina, routinely seizing slaves on plantations and coercing them into his Federal unit. According to Norwood P. Hallowell, who later commanded the all-black Fifty-Fifth Massachusetts Volunteer Regiment, Hunter's strong-armed recruiting tactics served "as an example of how not to do it."[22]

In August 1862, when Secretary of War Edwin M. Stanton refused to recognize and pay Hunter's black recruits, the general had no choice but to disband all but one company of his troops on duty on St. Simon's Island (its sergeant never received the order to disband).[23] At this point Lincoln made clear his public opposition to arming blacks, informing a "Deputation of Western Gentlemen" that he could not accept their offer to arm African Americans but would continue to employ them as laborers. It was a matter of timing, reported the *New York Herald*. "We are all rejoicing that 'Abe' refuses to accept the negroes as soldiers," wrote Illinois infantryman Charles W. Wills. "Aside from the immense disaffection it would create in our army, the South would arm and put in the field three negroes to our one." As his justification for not arming blacks, Lincoln asserted that "the nation could not afford to lose Kentucky at this crisis, and . . . that to arm the negroes would turn 50,000 bayonets from the loyal Border States against us that were for us." He used almost identical language in responding to a delegation of Chicago Christians on September 13, nine days before issuing his preliminary Emancipation Proclamation, but added: "I am not so sure we could do much with the blacks. If we were to arm them, I fear that in a few weeks the arms would be in the hands of the rebels; and indeed thus far we have not had arms enough to equip our white troops."[24]

That said, in September Secretary of War Stanton reversed the administration's policy, quietly authorizing General Rufus Saxton to begin recruiting black South Carolinians where Hunter had left off. Permitting Saxton to arm five thousand "volunteers of African descent," Stanton hoped to guard coastal plantations from Confederate marauders and to deny the Rebels laborers. Lincoln's early recruiting ventures served not only as experiments—testing white and black, Union and Confederate, public opinion to mobilizing African American soldiers—but also as stopgap measures to provide temporary influxes of troops where and when needed. Disgusted by what he considered Lincoln's circuitous and inconsistent approach to emancipation, abolitionist William Lloyd Garrison wrote his daughter: "The President can do nothing for *freedom* in a direct manner, but only by circumlocution and delay. How prompt was his action against Fremont [*sic*] and Hunter!"[25]

The success of recruiting efforts in Kansas, Louisiana, and South Carolina, however, moved Lincoln gradually toward recognizing the vital connection between redirecting the war effort by way of military emancipation. By October 1862, Saxton, with Hunter's lone company as its core, was organizing the First South Carolina Volunteers, the earliest regiment of ex-slaves recognized by the War Department, under the command of Colonel Thomas Wentworth Higginson. In November it participated in a coastal raid that freed more than 150 slaves. Other regiments of black South Carolinians soon followed. In March 1863 they led a large-scale action against Jacksonville, Florida.[26]

Much to Lincoln's displeasure, Hunter's unauthorized recruitment became hotly debated in Congress. In July 1862 Kentucky representatives Charles A. Wickliffe and Robert Mallory denounced Lincoln's administration for recruiting blacks without congressional authority. Wickliffe implored the president "to pause in this mad and impolitic scheme of emancipation." He added: "a negro is afraid, by instinct or by nature, of a gun. Give him a bowie-knife or a John Brown pike if you want to get up a servile war, of murder, conflagration, and rapine." Mallory declared that arming blacks was "contrary to the rules that should govern a civilized nation in conducting war." "I shrink from arming the slave, using him to shoot down white men, knowing his depraved nature as I do. I would as soon think of enlisting the Indian, and of arming him with the tomahawk and scalping knife, to be let loose upon our rebellious countrymen, as to arm the negro in this contest," he said.[27]

Congressman Thaddeus Stevens disagreed sharply with the Kentuckians. Ridiculing them, Stevens asked how white southerners could consider blacks "a savage and barbarous race, if one gun will disperse an army of them?" Throughout history, Stevens lectured Congress, nations at war had liberated slaves and employed them against their former masters, and the U.S. government should do so as well. Freeing and arming South Carolina slaves was essential, he argued, first to deprive the Confederacy of its labor, and second to replace white troops from serving in the pestilent, miasmatic low country. "I am for sending the Army through the whole slave population," Stevens explained, "and asking them to come from their masters, to take the weapons which we furnish, and to join us in this war of freedom against traitors and rebels." Once they were trained as soldiers, Stevens favored sending the black troops "to shooting their masters if they will not submit to this Government." "I do not view it as an abolition or as an emancipation question," he concluded. "I view it as the means, and the only means, of putting down this rebellion."[28]

Early on, Lincoln no doubt purposely gave mixed messages on mobilizing black troops because he hoped to defeat the Confederates and end slavery via different means. In order to retain the loyalty of the border slave states—Delaware, Kentucky, Maryland, and Missouri—and to respect the principle of private property, during the first eighteen months of the war he cautioned against taking "radical and extreme" steps. In November 1861 Lincoln presented a model for compensated emancipation in Delaware that he hoped each of the border states would embrace. It provided Federal compensation for slave owners, established an apprenticeship for minors, and ended slavery over a thirty-year period. Delaware legislators spurned this conservative emancipation program unequivocally.[29] In his December 1861 message to Congress, the president urged Congress to fund the repatriation of blacks freed by the First Confiscation Act, as well as northern free blacks who wished to leave the country. Lincoln pledged that his goal was "to keep the integrity of the Union prominent as the primary object of the contest."[30]

In early 1862, in the first emancipation initiative proposed by a U.S. president, Lincoln proffered using Federal funds to compensate loyal slaveholders for their bondsmen in the four border slave states.[31] On March 6 he outlined a compensated emancipation program, hoping that once the loyal slave states implemented the plan, it could be extended to each Confederate state as they succumbed to Union armies. Lincoln calculated that the cost of freeing the slaves in the border states would total less than the cost of continuing the war for eighty-seven days. Despite his pleas, border state leaders rejected Lincoln's appeal.[32] In May he again appealed to border state leaders, urging them not to "be blind to the signs of the times" by refusing emancipation. Compensated emancipation "would come gently as the dews of heaven," Lincoln prophesized, "not rending or wrecking anything. Will you not embrace it?"[33] None did.

The president had more success when in March 1862 Congress enacted an additional Article of War, rendering all but inoperable the Fugitive Slave Laws of 1793 and 1850. The article prohibited military and naval personnel from "returning fugitives from service or labor, who may have escaped from any persons to whom such service or labor is claimed to be due."[34] In April Congress abolished slavery in the District of Columbia, providing compensation to loyal slave owners of up to $300 for each freed slave, allocated $100,000 to assist persons of color who volunteered to settle in either Haiti or Liberia, and payments of up to $100 for each person choosing emigration. "I am gratified," Lincoln informed Congress after it passed the bill, "that the two principles of compensation and colonization are both recognized, and practically applied in the act."[35] He scored yet another victory in June when Congress emancipated slaves (but without compensating their masters) in the Federal territories.[36] This act overturned the notorious *Dred Scott v. Sanford* (1857) decision.

Still convinced of the importance of state-guided, compensated emancipation as a means of ending slavery gradually, on July 12, 1862, Lincoln met a third time with border state representatives and senators. Once more he urged the congressmen to accept reality. "The incidents of the war can not be avoided," the president explained, and slavery in their states would be extinguished "by mere friction and abrasion—by the mere incidents of the war." Lincoln urged the border state leaders to accept the government's financial offer before their property depreciated even more. "How much better for you, as seller, and the nation as buyer, to sell out, and buy out, that without which the war could never have been, than to sink both the thing to be sold, and the price of it, in cutting one another's throats." Lincoln's plan included compensated gradual emancipation and colonization in South America. Again a majority of border state leaders rejected Lincoln's appeal.[37]

Committed since the 1850s to colonization as the solution to America's "race problem," Lincoln suggested that physical differences between the races mandated that blacks and whites should be separated. Fearful that northern conservatives, especially border state Unionists, would equate freeing blacks with racial equality, Lincoln tied emancipation to colonization.[38] In his December 3, 1861, message to Congress, for example, Lincoln had recommended that black persons freed under the First Confiscation Act be resettled voluntarily "at some place, or places, in a climate congenial to them."[39] He had in mind the black republics of Haiti and Liberia, both of which gained official recognition during Lincoln's presidency.[40] But like Lincoln's plans to compensate Unionist slaveholders, his dreams to colonize freed blacks also came to naught. Following the rejection of his compensated emancipation plan by border state representatives, Lincoln decided to issue a presidential emancipation decree.

In mid-July 1862 the president's emancipation project received a major boost from Congress when it passed two bills linking the freeing of the slaves directly to military enlistment. The Militia Act (passed July 17, 1862, following General George B. McClellan's failed Peninsular Campaign) was a mélange of miscellaneous military provisions. Virginia slaves' multifaceted roles as laborers, hospital attendants, armed soldiers, and suppliers of military intelligence during McClellan's botched spring campaign caught the attention of Lincoln as well as many northerners, encouraging them toward emancipating and arming the slaves.[41] The bill emancipated Confederate bondsmen employed by the Union army (as well as their mothers, wives, and children), and authorized the president "to receive into the service of the United States, for the purpose of constructing intrenchments, or performing camp service, or any other labor, or any military or naval service for which they may be found competent, persons of African descent." The Militia Act also specified that African Americans employed by the military were to be paid "ten dollars per month and one ration, three dollars of which monthly pay may be in clothing."[42] Congress thus gave Lincoln the authority he required to arm black men, but it clearly intended the Militia Act to apply to slaves of disloyal owners, not northern free blacks or loyal border state slaveholders.[43]

Outraged that Lincoln seemingly was willing only to free slaves to work, not fight, in July Frederick Douglass charged that Lincoln's policies had "been calculated . . . to shield and protect slavery," and that the president had "scornfully rejected the policy of arming the slaves, a policy naturally suggested and enforced by the nature and necessities of the war." Two months later, in a blistering editorial Douglass branded Lincoln little more than "an itinerant Colonization lecturer, showing all his inconsistencies, his pride of race and blood, his contempt for Negroes and his canting hypocrisy." Despite the president's professed antislavery views, Douglass blasted him as "quite a genuine representative of American prejudice and Negro hatred and far more concerned for the preservation of slavery, and the favor of the Border Slave States, than for any sentiment of magnanimity or principle of justice and humanity." Douglass complained that Lincoln, lacking "courage and honesty," had failed to enforce the Second Confiscation Act, had "evaded his obvious duty, and instead of calling the blacks to arms and to liberty he merely authorized the military commanders to use them as laborers, without even promising them their freedom at the end of their term of service . . . and thus destroyed virtually the very object of the measure."[44]

The Second Confiscation Act (also passed on July 17, 1862) was stronger in intent than its predecessor and resembled Frémont's 1861 proclamation that Lincoln had rescinded. If the Confederates did not surrender in sixty days, the new confiscation bill authorized Federal courts to free the slaves of persons "engaged in rebellion" and empowered the president "to employ as many persons of African descent as he may deem necessary and proper for the suppression of this rebellion, and for this purpose he may organize and use them in such manner as he may judge best for the public welfare." While Congress had smoothed the way for freeing Rebels' slaves and for deploying bondsmen as Federal soldiers, the legislation applied only to states in rebellion, guaranteed the return of runaway slaves to loyal border state slaveholders, offered blacks no guarantee of civil or political rights, and gave the president authority to resettle, "in some tropical country . . . such persons of the African race, made free by the provisions of this act, as may be willing to emigrate, having first obtained the consent of the government of said country."[45]

Despite its limitations, contemporaries grasped the importance of the Second Confiscation Act as an instrument of military emancipation. The *Oberlin Evangelist* predicted, "No measure would panic-smite the rebels like this. An earnest proclamation from President Lincoln calling every able-bodied slave in the seceded States to arms and offering freedom as the bounty—freedom to his mother, wife and children—would appall Jeff. Davis and all his confederates, would scatter his armed legions to their homes and soon end the war." Editor Henry Cowles implored Lincoln to stop placating border state slaveholders and change the spiritless, rudderless direction of the war by arming the South's slaves. "Let us have a new programme, and at the head of it, colored regiments!" Deploying black troops, he said, would offer the Union multiple benefits, denying the Confederates slave labor, killing the "peculiar institution," and augmenting depleted Union ranks with men especially eager to fight the Rebels. Cowles interpreted the arming of the slaves as a millennial move that would uplift the South's bondsmen, instilling in them discipline, and raising them "from imbecility to courage and power." Once trained and mobilized the black soldiers "will dare to think themselves men—and this is one long step towards their becoming such." For these reasons and others, the editor wrote, "Black regiments are the arm of the Almighty to divide the issue of this rebellion."[46] In far off San Francisco, Philip A. Bell, the black editor of the *Pacific Appeal*, also welcomed the new Confiscation Act, interpreting it as a bridge to arming the men of his race. "The Negro," he wrote, "is at last acknowledged as a part of that effective force of the country: not the fighting force, it is true, but the working force: the other must naturally follow, for they who construct entrenchments, build fortifications and perform any kind of military or naval service, will soon be called upon to defend, by arms, the forts, camps and ships wherein they are employed as servants."[47]

Lincoln, however, found the Second Confiscation Act less promising as an instrument of emancipation. In practice it liberated only those slaves who belonged to "traitors" as determined by case-by-case litigation by the Federal courts, and he doubted its constitutionality. With these reservations the president signed the bill only reluctantly. The law was "prospective" in intent, serving as a warning of future punishments rather than instituting immediate retribution.[48] Poorly crafted, cumbersome, and difficult to implement, the Second Confiscation Act depended on the U.S. courts for enforcement, and Congress provided no funds to implement it. Not surprisingly, Lincoln generally neglected the two Confiscation Acts, and his government confiscated little Rebel property.[49] Determined to provide a more workable solution to the question of slaves as property, the president devised his own process for emancipation, one that ultimately included black recruitment.

Heretofore Lincoln had considered only gradual, compensated, and voluntary emancipation. But faced with the cumbersome Second Confiscation Act, between July and September 1862 the president developed a "two-track policy, carefully distinguishing between the type of emancipation appropriate for loyal regions and the procedure to be dictated in areas still rebelling against government authority." And whereas the congressional law seemingly would treat emancipation one case at a time, Lincoln promised to free slaves in an entire sub-region with one stroke of his pen, targeting not just Confederate troops but Rebel civilians and their property as well.[50]

On July 21, 1862, four days after signing the Militia and Second Confiscation Acts, the president met with his cabinet, informing them of his intent to implement the emancipation and military provisions of the acts, but not colonization. Though his cabinet favored another proposal by General David Hunter to enlist black soldiers, Lincoln demurred. The following day he shared with his cabinet what became the preliminary Emancipation Proclamation. Lincoln's new measure went beyond the Second Confiscation Act (which did not apply to most Confederate slaves until they came under Federal control) by extending wartime emancipation to the locales where most Confederate slaves resided. Abolition would result immediately and not include compensation. The loyalty of the slave owner would be irrelevant.[51] And emancipation would be a war measure, a presidential edict, enabling Lincoln to circumvent Capitol Hill and the Federal courts.

Secretary of the Treasury Salmon P. Chase reported that at the July 22 cabinet meeting, Lincoln opposed arming black men, a practice that he believed "would be productive of more evil than good." But the president nevertheless "was not unwilling that Commanders should, at their discretion, arm, for purely defensive purposes, slaves coming within their lines." Chase added that Lincoln "proposed to issue a Proclamation, on the basis of the Confiscation Bill, calling upon the States to return to their allegiance . . . and proclaiming the emancipation of all slaves within States remaining in insurrection on the first of January, 1863." Thus originated the first formal draft of what became the preliminary Emancipation Proclamation.[52]

Though Chase no doubt noted correctly Lincoln's attitudes toward military recruitment, the subject preoccupied him. On or around July 22 the president drafted a Memorandum on Recruiting Negroes that consisted of five points:

> To recruiting free negroes, no objection.
> To recruiting slaves of disloyal owners, no objection.
> To recruiting slaves of loyal owners *with their consent*, no objection.
> To recruiting slaves of loyal owners *without* consent, objection, *unless the necessity is urgent.*
> To concluding offensively, while recruiting, and to carrying away slaves not suitable for recruits, objection.[53]

The president's words thus make clear that two months before issuing the preliminary Emancipation Proclamation, and more than four months before approving black enlistment, Lincoln's only objections to arming slaves concerned those belonging to loyal slaveholders, to what he obliquely termed "concluding offensively, while recruiting," and to the enlistment of bondsmen unsuited for military service. For political reasons, however, especially his fear of alienating Kentuckians, Lincoln chose not to unveil his position on recruiting African Americans and waited until the new year to authorize their enlistment as a war measure. As it turned out, Democrats capitalized on the explosiveness and unpopularity of the preliminary Emancipation Proclamation in the fall 1862 by-elections, thumping Republicans at the polls and stoking the fires of negrophobia. The Republicans' control of Congress was tenuous at best.[54]

As January 1 approached, Lincoln prepared Americans for the reality of emancipation but continued to give no indication that he would arm the slaves. In his December 1862 annual message to Congress, the president revived old strategies, proposing three constitutional amendments for voluntary and compensated emancipation by 1900 with colonization. He urged the "friends of the Union" to settle their differences over slavery. "Without slavery," he reminded Americans, "the rebellion could never have existed; without slavery it could not continue."[55] Apparently believing that Lincoln had yet to make up his mind about enlisting blacks, on New Year's Eve Treasury Secretary Chase urged him not to include a clause initiating the enlistment of black men in his final proclamation. Arming the slaves was unnecessary, Chase maintained. He preferred following "the natural course of things already well begun." The best means of suppressing the rebellion was to draw upon "the organized military force of the loyal population of the insurgent regions, of whatever complexion." He doubted that mobilizing slaves into the Union army would prevent "irregular violence and servile insurrection" by "those who might otherwise probably resort to such courses."[56]

Sixteen months after issuing his final proclamation Lincoln explained why he had changed course. Writing to Kentucky editor Albert G. Hodges, the president recalled that when in the spring and summer of 1862 he had "made earnest, and successive appeals to the border states to favor compensated emancipation," he already believed that "the indispensable necessity for military emancipation, and arming the blacks would come, unless averted by that measure." When the border states rejected his proposals, Lincoln continued, he was "driven to the alternative of either surrendering the Union, and with it, the Constitution, or of laying strong hand upon the colored element. I chose the latter." Lincoln admitted that he came to the conclusion pragmatically. "In choosing it, I hoped for greater gain than loss; but of this, I was not entirely confident." The need to fill depleted units, the necessity of employing the thousands of fugitive slaves who had entered Federal lines, and the compulsion to deprive vital manpower from the insurgents convinced Lincoln in late 1862 that the time was indeed right to free the Confederacy's slaves and to arm black men, north and south.[57]

No one proved more enthusiastic over Lincoln's transformation than Douglass, who just months before had lambasted Lincoln over what he considered his lethargy in freeing and arming the slaves. The fiery abolitionist marveled at the "amazing change" in the president's emancipation policy—"this amazing approximation toward the sacred truth of human liberty." "We are all liberated," by the Emancipation Proclamation, Douglass said. "The white man is liberated, the black man is liberated, the brave men now fighting the battles of their country against rebels and traitors are now liberated, and may strike . . . the Rebels, at their most sensitive point." The destruction of slavery had become a military necessity for Lincoln and a major Union war aim.[58]

Others shared such sentiments. For example, General John White Geary, a Union army brigade commander, remarked, "The President's proclimation [sic] is the most important public document ever issued by an officer of our Government, and although I believe it, in itself, to be correct, I tremble for the consequences." Responding to newspaper reports of Lincoln's proclamation, another officer of antislavery convictions, Lieutenant John Quincy Adams Campbell of the Fifth Iowa Infantry, proclaimed January 1, 1863, "the day of our nation's second birth. God bless and help Abraham Lincoln—help him to 'break every yoke and let the oppressed go free.' The President has placed the Union pry under the corner stone of the Confederacy and the structure *will* fall." In a pamphlet circulated widely in the North, George H. Boker proclaimed: "We are raising a black army. We are thus incurring a solemn obligation to abolish slavery wherever our flag flies. . . . When we do this, we shall have taken the last step in our difficult path, and shall have reached the goal, the natural, inevitable, fitting and triumphant end of the war, *emancipation*—the one essential condition to peace and Union."[59]

* * *

The president's final Emancipation Proclamation ratified important steps toward military emancipation taken by Congress over the previous year, most notably the Militia and Second Confiscation Acts. Lincoln's military decree, however, made emancipation explicitly an official war aim, declaring free all slaves in the Confederate South with the temporary exception of Tennessee and Union-occupied southern Louisiana and tidewater Virginia. As Union armies marched southward, they came as torchbearers of freedom.

To be sure, the final document had limitations, as its critics, then and now, have noted. A Mississippi humorist, neither friend of emancipation nor fan of the president, composed a disparaging ditty: "Abraham Lincoln, the wily wretch. Freed the slaves he couldn't catch."[60] Lincoln's military edict applied only to the Confederacy, essentially areas beyond Union control. It had no bearing on almost one-half million slaves in the four loyal border states and West Virginia. It exempted areas already occupied by Federal troops, including seven counties in Tidewater Virginia, thirteen parishes in southern Louisiana, and all of Tennessee. Approximately three hundred thousand slaves resided in these areas. Altogether, then, the president's proclamation exempted about eight hundred thousand of the country's 3.9 million slaves. And the document depended on the Union army to give it any muscle.[61]

Lincoln's proclamation, however, did in fact free many slaves along the Mississippi River, in eastern North and South Carolina, on the Sea Islands along the Atlantic coast, and in pockets throughout the Confederacy occupied by Federal armies. Nonetheless his critics have interpreted the restrained, legalistic wording of the Emancipation Proclamation as indicative of Lincoln's overall lethargy in freeing and arming the slaves; they complained that he continually equivocated, that he followed others and rarely defined policy himself.[62]

Unlike the president, his critics did not have to worry about maintaining Republican political support in state and national elections during an increasingly unpopular war amid complaints, especially in the border states, of Federal usurpation of power. On September

25, 1862, for example, the fiery Garrison remarked, "The President's Proclamation is certainly matter for great rejoicing . . . but it leaves slavery, as a system or practice, still to exist in all the so-called loyal Slave States, under the old constitutional guaranties, even to slave-hunting in the Free States, in accordance with the wicked Fugitive Slave Law." The old abolitionist found Lincoln's decree wanting. "What was wanted, what is still needed," he exclaimed, "is a procla-mation, distinctly announcing the total abolition of slavery." Unitar-ian minister Moncure D. Conway agreed, faulting Lincoln for not going far enough in his final proclamation and for failing to make the war a moral crusade against slavery. Conway came away from a meeting with Lincoln in January 1863 "with a conviction that the practical success of the Emancipation Proclamation was by no means certain in the hands of the author."[63]

Sergeant George E. Stephens, who would join the all-black Fifty-Fourth Massachusetts Volunteers, the first African American regiment recruited in the North, also questioned Lincoln's intentions. Early in the war the freeborn Pennsylvanian had served as an officer's servant in the Army of the Potomac and became an incisive observer and critic of Lincoln's emancipation policies. Though on New Year's Eve, 1862, Stephens predicted that the Emancipation Proclamation would wash away "the sorrows, tears, and anguish of millions" and "necessitate a general arming of the freedmen," Lincoln's actions quickly soured him on the president.[64] Though once they had the chance, many black men like Stephens rushed to join the USCT, African Americans across the North debated whether they should enlist immediately or wait until Lincoln's government recognized their manhood and citi-zenship. These "conversations about enlistment suggested that black men fought not to restore the old Union but to bring forth a new, reformed Union in which they could live fully as men and citizens."[65]

Like other critics, black and white, Stephens chided Lincoln for moving too slowly to free the slaves, for acting on military, not humanitarian grounds, and for leaving the "peculiar institution" untouched along the borderland. Stephens resented that in his pre-liminary proclamation, the president attempted to convince the Confederacy into surrendering by allowing its slaveholders to retain their bondsmen. "The Emancipation proclamation," Stephens wrote in the *New York Weekly Anglo-African*, "should have been based as much on the righteousness of emancipation as on the great need of the measure, and then let the people see that the war for slavery and secession could be vigorously met only by war for the Union against slavery." As late as September 1864, Stephens condemned Lincoln's military emancipation project as "the fulmination of one man, by virtue of his military authority, who proposes to free the slaves of that portion of territory over which he has no control, while those portions of slave territory under control of the Union armies is exempted, and slavery receives as much protection as it ever did. United States officers and soldiers are yet employed hunting fugitive slaves." He further damned Lincoln's proclamation as "an abortion wrung from the Executive womb by necessity."[66]

Some northerners, including white racists and those who opposed the military draft, supported the president's proclamation because it provided a means of filling Union regiments without sacrificing yet more white men. Such reasoning, according to Joseph T. Wilson, an African American who served with two USCT regiments, represented the "not unnatural willingness of the white soldiers to allow the negro troops to stop the bullets that they would otherwise have to receive." "When this war is over & we have summed up the entire loss of life it has imposed," Iowa Governor Samuel J. Kirkwood wrote, "I shall not have any regrets if it is found that a part of the dead are *niggers* and that *all* are not white men."[67]

Whereas some complained that Lincoln's emancipation policies fell too short, others judged them as going too far. The president's final Emancipation Proclamation aroused racial fears across white communities and elicited much criticism throughout the North. Critics denounced it as radical and revolutionary. They charged that the twin calamities of black emancipation and military recruitment would unleash, among other catastrophes, race war, miscegenation, disaffection in the North, and heightened resistance by the Confederates.

Though opposed to slavery because it contradicted "the spirit of modern progress and civilization," Massachusetts's Charles Francis Adams Jr., grandson of President John Quincy Adams and son of

U.S. diplomat Charles Francis Adams, nonetheless believed that emancipation would ultimately harm the freedpeople. He predicted that it would open the South's cotton fields to free labor and modern technology, thereby destroying the slaves' "value as agricultural machines." "As to being made soldiers," Adams insisted, "they are more harm than good." At best they could perform "fatigue" or labor duty. "It will be years before they can be made to stand before their old masters, unless . . . some leader of their own, some Toussaint [L'Ouverture] rises, who is one of them and inspires them with confidence. Under our system and with such white officers as we give them, we might make a soldierly equal to the native Hindoo regiments in about five years." Black recruitment would prove too costly, Adams said, and "arming the blacks *as soldiers* must be abandoned."[68] Ironically Adams, because of his deep hatred of slavery, later commanded the all-black Fifth Massachusetts Cavalry.

Like Adams, early in the war many white northern soldiers doubted the blacks' abilities to fight and protested against Lincoln's program of freeing and arming them. Some were ambivalent over the president's policies. Others expressed feelings of anger and betrayal. Willing to sacrifice their lives to suppress the rebellion, they had not joined the army to liberate black people or to serve alongside them in the army. The pioneer African American historian George Washington Williams, a USCT veteran, wrote in 1887 that the black soldier entered the war surrounded by prejudice and bad faith, "persistently denied public confidence." At best white troops "damned him with faint praise— with elevated eyebrows and elaborate pantomime. The good words of the conscientious few who felt . . . that he would fight were drowned by a babel of wrathful depreciation of him as a man and as a soldier."[69]

For example, shortly after Lincoln issued his preliminary proclamation Lieutenant George Washington Whitman, the poet's brother, of the Fifty-First New York Volunteers, remarked: "I dont know what effect it is going to have on the war, but one thing is certain, he [Lincoln] has got to lick the south before he can free the niggers . . . and unless he drives ahead and convinces the south . . . that we are bound to lick them, and it would be better for them to behave themselvs and keep their slaves, than to get licked and lose them, I dont think the proclamation will do much good." Another soldier, Corporal George W. Squier of the Forty-Fourth Indiana Volunteers, predicted that the Emancipation Proclamation would have a deleterious effect on Union troops. Although Squier considered the proclamation "in itself right and intende[d] for good," he believed that it would "add one hundred thousand men to the rebbels' army and take nearly as many *from* our army." Squier found Kentucky troops particularly unwilling "to peril their lives to, as they say free the 'Nigger,' and many, very many from the free states are little better."[70]

Major Henry Livermore Abbott of the Twentieth Massachusetts Volunteers strongly opposed emancipation and expressed sentiments common among officers in the Army of the Potomac. Soon after the final Emancipation Proclamation went into effect, Livermore informed his aunt: "The president's proclamation is of course received with universal disgust, particularly the part which enjoins officers to see that it is carried out. You may be sure that we shan't see to any thing of the kind." Another soldier, Corporal Thomas H. Mann of the Eighteenth Massachusetts Volunteers, noted succinctly, "The President's Proc[lamation] will have *no* effect except in conquered territory . . . [and] will prolong the war." Faced with the prospect of serving with black soldiers, Corporal Felix Brannigan of the Seventy-Fourth New York Volunteers, wrote his sister: "We don't want to fight side and side with the nigger." He asserted: "We think we are a too superior race for that."[71]

Sergeant Symmes Stillwell of the Ninth New Jersey Volunteers concurred. He considered arming the slaves to be "a confession of weakness, a folly, an insult to the brave Solder." William C. H. Reeder, a private in the Twentieth Indiana Volunteers, refused to reenlist because, he said, "this war has turned out very Different from what I thought it would. . . . It is a War . . . to free the Nigars . . . and I do not propose to fight any more in such A cause." Soon after Lincoln's final emancipation edict went into effect, Henry Phelps Hubbell of the Third New York Volunteers threatened to quit the army, disgusted by the president's policy toward African Americans. "I would sooner see every nigger now free, *in* slavery," he informed his brother, "than see slavery abolished." "Talk about 'honest Old

Abe,'" Hubbell grumbled, "I believe that he is as big a scoundrel as any of them."[72]

In July 1864 Lincoln found himself in the uncomfortable position of having to ask one of his most capable field commanders, General William T. Sherman, well known for his antipathy toward black people and his opposition to military emancipation, for his "hearty co-operation" in allowing northern agents to recruit African Americans near his camps. Two months later Sherman complained against emancipation and black recruitment. "I dont see why we cant have some sense about negros," he wrote, "as well as about horses mules, iron, copper &c.—but Say nigger in the U.S. and . . . the whole country goes Crazy. . . . I like niggers *well enough* as niggers, but when fools & idiots try & make niggers better than ourselves I have an opinion." Three months before Appomattox, Sherman again groused that northern radicals had become obsessed with "Sambo." "The South deserves all she has got for her injustice to the negro," Sherman admitted, "but that is no reason why we should go to the other extreme."[73]

Such comments underscore the degree to which Lincoln's final proclamation had indeed transformed the war from a constitutional struggle over the maintenance of the Union to one of black freedom. Though many northerners, the president included, wondered whether forced manumissions by the government would be tested in the courts following the war, most persons agreed that wartime emancipation signaled the death knell of slavery. African Americans would be "forever free."[74]

To effect that change Lincoln ushered in the first large-scale use of black men as combat soldiers in American history. According to Colonel Higginson, the president's decision to arm African Americans was "a momentous experiment, whose ultimate results were the reorganization of the whole American army & the remoulding of the relations of two races on this continent." After 1863 black men, free and slave, rushed to join Lincoln's army, determined to bury slavery, to defeat the Confederates, to prove their manhood, and to earn full citizenship. "We came out in 1[8]63," a black soldier recalled, "as Valent hearted men for the Sacke of our Surffring Courntury."

Many, like Georgian Hubbard Pryor of the Forty-Fourth USCT, escaped from slavery, entered Federal lines, and enlisted in the Federal service. When the Rebels captured Pryor in Dalton, Georgia, in October 1864, they reenslaved him. He spent the remainder of the war working on Confederate labor gangs in Alabama, Mississippi, and southwest Georgia.[75]

Significantly, Lincoln premised his final Emancipation Proclamation on "military necessity." And though the legalistic provision arming the slaves appeared as but an afterthought, Lincoln's text provided a stunning new role—as Union troops—for newly freed slaves and northern free blacks. No longer, to use Douglass's terms would African Americans be "confined to the outer margin of the rebellion."[76] As soldiers they fought and died alongside white men and personified the president's commitment to black freedom.

EMANCIPATION AND MOBILIZATION

News of Abraham Lincoln's final Emancipation Proclamation spread quickly across Union army camps in occupied areas of the Confederacy, where Federal officers read the document aloud to white troops and contrabands alike. Black people in coastal South Carolina, upon listening to Lincoln's words, simultaneously began singing "My Country, 'Tis of Thee." In Virginia the men of the Eleventh Corps heard news of the proclamation from their officers. So too did African Americans in the vicinity who responded to the document "with great jubilation." Gossip of Lincoln's military emancipation edict also filtered down to bonds people on farms and plantations across the Confederacy. Slaves on a Virginia plantation belonging to a Confederate sympathizer reportedly threw down their tools and halted work. Soon thousands of others would shoulder rifles instead.[1]

To mobilize black recruits Philadelphia's Supervisory Committee for Recruiting Colored Regiments published a two-sided handbill that captured not only the symbolism of military emancipation during the war, but also the binary nature of the perennial historical question "who freed the slaves?" One side contains a recruiting poster calling blacks to arms, to free their slave brethren, to reunite the nation, and to stand as equals with whites. The poster reads: "All slaves were made Freemen by Abraham Lincoln, President of the United States, January 1st, 1863. Come, then, able-bodied Colored Men, to the nearest United States Camp, and fight for the Stars and

Stripes." The reverse side of the poster is a richly colored lithograph entitled *Freedom to the Slave*. An African American male, an officer with shoulder straps and dress sash, stands at the center of the print, glancing toward the heavens. Others—black soldiers, slaves, and presumably freedmen—surround the USCT officer.[2]

Lincoln's final Emancipation Proclamation ushered in the first mobilization of African American soldiers in U.S. history. In inviting black men to bear arms to suppress the rebellion, Lincoln opened dramatic new avenues to freedom and manhood. The establishment of the USCT in 1863 became the focal point of the president's emancipation project, and his subordinates worked to systematize and integrate black recruitment into national policy. In a widely circulated pamphlet the Philadelphia publisher Henry Carey Baird urged politicians to enlist black troops immediately. "By utilizing this element the Government can secure the services of 700,000 able-bodied men, acclimated to and familiar with the seat of war, and at the same time strike the Rebels a vital blow."[3]

Frederick Douglass concurred, arguing in February 1863, "Whoever sees fifty thousand well drilled colored soldiers in the United States, will see slavery abolished and the union of these States secured from rebel violence." A month later Lincoln confided to General Nathaniel P. Banks that he considered the raising of black troops "very important, if not indispensable." "The colored population is the great *available* and yet *unavailed* of, force for restoring the Union," the president informed Military Governor Andrew Johnson of Tennessee. "The bare sight of fifty thousand armed, and drilled black soldiers on the banks of the Mississippi, would end the rebellion at once."[4] Lincoln professed that mobilizing black troops in the Volunteer State also would help Johnson in drafting a new state constitution for Tennessee and in establishing a loyal government there.[5]

In May 1863 Lincoln responded favorably to a proposal from a committee of New Yorkers who urged him to give General John C. Frémont command of ten thousand black troops recruited in the North. Lincoln replied, saying that he would welcome "not ten thousand but ten times ten thousand colored troops," and pledged himself to protecting those who enlisted and "looked to them for essential service in finishing the war."[6] In a widely printed letter to his Springfield confidante James C. Conkling, the president reiterated a point he would make many times—that no matter what happened during and after the war, emancipation would stand. Military and political events would not undo the Union's commitment to emancipation. Black people, he explained, "like other people, act upon motives. Why should they do anything for us, if we will do nothing for them? If they stake their lives for us, they must be prompted by the strongest motive—even the promise of freedom. And the promise being made, must be kept."[7]

By August 1863, when black troops already had proven their mettle under fire, Lincoln addressed those who criticized his decision to arm the black men. The president remarked that some of his commanders, including those who opposed abolition and the Republicans, had become strong supporters of emancipation and the recruitment of blacks. "You say you will not fight to free negroes," the president declared, adding wryly, "Some of them are willing to fight for you." The following year Lincoln recalled that he experimented with arming free blacks in the North and former slaves in the South with "a clear conviction of duty . . . to turn that element of strength to account; and I am responsible for it to the American people, to the Christian world, to history, and on my final account, to God."[8]

* * *

Once Lincoln's proclamation went into effect, Secretary of War Edwin M. Stanton sprang into action. He authorized Massachusetts, Rhode Island, and Connecticut to commence recruiting black regiments. Massachusetts governor John A. Andrew moved quickly, and within weeks black volunteers from throughout the North began enlisting in the Fifty-Fourth Massachusetts Volunteers. Lincoln's administration also dispatched sympathetic Union officers, including Generals Daniel Ullmann and Edward A. Wild, to go south, to Louisiana and North Carolina, respectively, to raise regiments of slaves. Colonel James Montgomery began recruiting in South Carolina, while recruiters soon canvassed other New England and Midwestern states to recruit all-black volunteer regiments.

Prominent black and white abolitionists, including Douglass, George L. Stearns, Richard P. Hallowell, Martin R. Delany, William Birney, Henry McNeal Turner, and John Mercer Langston, soon traversed the North gathering recruits. The War Department instructed them to return the men to New England, where they would be credited to the various states' draft quotas. When Langston, an African American, sought authorization from Ohio governor David Tod to recruit black soldiers in the state, Tod explained: "Do you not know, Mr. Langston, that this is a *white man's* government; that white men are able to defend and protect it, and that to enlist a negro soldier would be to drive every white man out of the service? When we want you colored men we will notify you." To this Langston replied: "Governor, when you need us, send for us."[9]

On January 10 Lincoln informed Stanton and Secretary of the Navy Gideon Welles that he wanted to move forward in recruiting blacks but to keep them out of harm's way—positioning them in posts where they would not be captured by Confederates and, as the Rebels threatened, executed. Accordingly Lincoln suggested to Stanton that they be assigned garrison duty (as per the wording of the final Emancipation Proclamation) at Memphis, Tennessee, Columbus, Kentucky, and other places, thereby allowing white soldiers to "go on more active service."[10]

Two days later congressman Thaddeus Stevens introduced a bill in the House of Representatives authorizing the president to raise 125,000 black soldiers. The slaves enlisted would become free, so too their families, and the government would compensate loyal slaveholders. Stevens' bill stalled in Congress, where Democrats and border state Unionists resorted to all manner of racist symbols and parliamentary tactics to block it. In fact, the 1862 Militia Act gave Lincoln all the authority he needed to recruit blacks with or without Congress's blessing. But the president feared that the U.S. Supreme Court might declare the bill unconstitutional.[11]

In March 1863 Lincoln, determined to have black men perform more than garrison duty, launched a major recruitment campaign in occupied areas of the Confederacy. Congress finally authorized the conscription of northern free blacks when it passed the controversial

Enrollment Act, rendering the enrollment, and possible draft, of "all able-bodied male citizens liable to perform military duty," and establishing a modern system of military conscription directed on the Federal level by Provost Marshal General James B. Fry.[12] As northern regiments began to fill with free blacks, Stanton authorized state governors to send more than one thousand agents to Louisiana, North Carolina, and the Mississippi Valley to recruit slaves in occupied territory. Douglass dramatically admonished black men "to fly to arms, and smite with death the power that would bury the government and your liberty in the same hopeless grave." His dream of "carrying the war into Africa" had become reality.[13]

Along with passing the Enrollment Act, in March 1863 Stanton took a major step toward recruiting slaves along the Confederate border by sending Adjutant General Lorenzo Thomas to the Mississippi Valley on an inspection tour, to begin the recruitment of blacks, and to identify whites—both officers and enlisted men—who might serve as officers of African American units. Stanton ordered Thomas to promote the government's new policy, begin its organization, and then leave the recruiting and training to officers in the field.[14]

As General Thomas headed west, Stanton instructed him to inform generals in the Mississippi Valley of the president's commitment to using blacks both as laborers and as armed soldiers. Black recruits were "to be provided with supplies upon the requisition of the proper officers, and in the same manner as other troops in the service." They would receive the same rations, uniforms, and equipment as white soldiers. Clearly, Lincoln envisioned a broader role for the USCT beyond the manning of outposts and performing fatigue labor as per the final Emancipation Proclamation.[15]

Overcoming all manner of racism within the ranks, Thomas succeeded in recruiting freedmen, in encouraging white noncommissioned officers to apply for commissions in black units, and in popularizing the employment of black soldiers. Though Thomas's men sometimes seized slaves and forced them into military service, he insisted that blacks be treated equally with whites and that African American regiments not be singled out for a disproportionate share of fatigue duty. In the spring of 1863, Samuel Evans, a newly minted lieutenant in the Fifty-Ninth USCT, explained the manner in which the army enlisted blacks in Moscow, in southwestern Tennessee. "The way we recruit [is to] mount a squad of about 50 men, ride out into the country where the darkies are, take all the negros (able bodied), all their mules (able bodied) and any gun that can be found in the hands of Citizens." Evans reported that during their training the black recruits were held to a higher discipline than white troops and learned to drill quickly. He predicted that they would prove to be effective combat soldiers. By May 1, Thomas had mustered his first regiment into service—the First Arkansas Volunteers of African Descent.[16]

Thomas took a second trip to the Mississippi Valley in August 1863. With that success in mind, Lincoln informed General Ulysses S. Grant that he believed African American units would become an invaluable "resource which, if vigorously applied now, will soon close the contest. It works doubly," he said, "weakening the enemy and strengthening us. We were not fully ripe for it until the [Mississippi] river was opened. Now, I think at least a hundred thousand [black soldiers] can, and ought to be rapidly organized along it's [*sic*] shores, relieving all the white troops to serve elsewhere." The president mentioned to Grant that Assistant Secretary of War Charles A. Dana had reported that the general believed "that the emancipation proclamation" had benefited his military operations. "I am very glad if this is so," Lincoln added.[17]

For his part Grant informed Lincoln that he heartily supported arming blacks. "This," he wrote, "with the emancipation of the negro, is the heavyest blow yet given the Confederacy." The Rebels no longer could divert their entire white male population to the military; the slaves were now less tractable. The general explained to Lincoln that Confederate cavalry were forcing slaves on each side of the Mississippi River eastward to Georgia and westward to Texas, making recruitment of "able bodied negroes" difficult. To remedy this problem Grant launched two expeditions into the Confederate interior accompanied by recruiting officers specifically targeting black recruits. The general reaffirmed his commitment to arming black men. In his opinion, "by arming the negro we have added a powerfully ally. They will make good soldiers and taking them from the enemy weaken him in the same proportion they strengthen us."[18]

In late August Grant provided detailed instructions to his commander in Natchez, General Marcellus M. Crocker, as to how Lincoln's administration wanted recruiting of black troops to be conducted. Federal recruiters were to differentiate between "Southern Citizens who have been loyal and those who have not; also a distinction between those who have not been loyal but now, express a voluntary willingness to return to their allegiance . . . and those who hold out in their acknowledgment of a Souther [*sic*] Confederacy." Clearly Lincoln sought to use the recruiting of slaves into the army to punish disloyal southerners and to increase the size of his army. Slaves belonging to Unionists were to be recruited, Grant explained, in the same manner as whites. They would enlist voluntarily. Slaves belonging to former Rebels were to be given the option of joining the USCT or not. But bondsmen held by Confederates or southern sympathizers could be "taken to put in the ranks." Grant suggested that recruiters compile lists of loyal and disloyal planters, cautioning Crocker, "In hunting them up the plantations of persons of known loyalty should not be visited."[19] By year's end General Thomas had organized twenty black regiments. By war's end he had participated in raising seventy such units, more than 40 percent of the USCT.[20]

* * *

During the first half of 1863, most recruiting for the USCT occurred in the deep South and the northeast. Though Lincoln eagerly sought black recruits from the border states (and authorized Stanton to recruit in Kentucky, Maryland, and Missouri), he proceeded carefully, knowing that white Kentuckians in particular deeply resented emancipation and the prospect of black Union soldiers. Slaveholders there were intensely committed to the "peculiar institution" and to white supremacy and clung tenaciously to the privileges of states' rights to protect them both.

Military emancipation posed serious challenges for Lincoln in the border slave states, where the freeing and arming of slaves belonging to Unionists became among the president's most contentious political-military dilemmas of the war. Because the final Emancipation Proclamation and its military recruitment provision did not apply to Delaware, Kentucky, Maryland, and Missouri, the army provided slaves the most direct legal path to freedom. Military enlistment in the border slave states tested Lincoln's commitment to emancipation beyond the specific terms of his proclamation, first in Maryland and then, more seriously, in his home state, Kentucky.[21]

In July 1863 Lincoln first authorized the recruitment of free blacks and slaves confiscated from Rebel masters in Baltimore, expanding the program to include slaves from throughout Maryland. He placed the recruiting efforts under Colonel William Birney, commander of the Twenty-Second USCT, and son of abolitionist James G. Birney. To appease Maryland slave owners the War Department credited black recruits to the state's draft quota, a policy that it later adopted in the other border states. Soon Governor Augustus W. Bradford complained loudly to Lincoln that Federal recruiters were seizing slaves of Unionists illegally. In October Stanton formulated rules, specifying that free blacks, slaves of Unionists with their owners' consent, and slaves of Rebels without their owners' consent could be inducted into the army in all the border states except Kentucky (temporarily exempted by Lincoln's government). Loyal masters would receive up to $300 compensation per slave. The slaves would be freed.[22]

Despite these rules, reports reached Lincoln in October—when the War Department ordered black recruitment to commence officially in Delaware, Maryland, and Missouri—that recruiters, including "armed colored troops," visited Maryland farms on the Patuxent River inducing slaves, regardless of their masters' allegiance, to enlist in Federal units. Lincoln contacted General Robert C. Schenck, his commander in Baltimore, demanding to know why the USCT were "frightening quiet people, and producing great confusion."[23] The president's secretary John Hay wrote that Lincoln favored voluntary enlistment of slaves with compensation for their owners, not their forcible seizure. Lincoln reportedly considered Schenck "wider across the head in the region of the ears, & [one who] loves fight for its own sake."[24] The president rightly worried about the political fallout from clashes between overly zealous military recruiters and Unionists in the border states; the problem continued until the end of the war. Recruiters frequently disregarded or simply failed to enquire whether slaves belonged to loyal or Rebel masters.

White Kentuckians resisted black recruitment most forcefully, even threatening rebellion if Lincoln pursued it in their commonwealth. The subject served as a rallying cry for Lincoln's opponents in Kentucky, whose obsession with the USCT "was little short of hysterical."[25] Colonel Frank Wolford, a popular officer of the First Kentucky Union Cavalry, protested Lincoln's policy of recruiting blacks so forcefully, urging Kentuckians to defy the president, that the army eventually discharged him dishonorably on the grounds of disloyalty.[26] In March 1864 Kentucky Union troops opened fire on Michigan soldiers because they had posted a "mulatto" to stand guard. The commander of the Kentuckians informed his Michigan counterpart, "If [the mulatto guard] was not immediately removed there would be trouble, as his men would not suffer a nigger soldier to be on duty in their presence."[27]

Over time the recruitment of USCT in Kentucky became a major problem for his administration, one that preoccupied Lincoln. Kentucky slaveholders assumed correctly that mobilization of the slaves would destroy slavery in their state, and accordingly they feverishly sought to circumvent or delay it. For his part, Lincoln worked to retain the loyalty and trust of his border state brethren. They tested Lincoln's patience and good will, even when he adopted as moderate a policy as possible toward them, treating Kentuckians "with kid gloves."[28] In practice, however, it seemed that the more the president tried to appease Kentucky's loyalist slaveholders, the more his efforts failed, exacerbating serious tensions between Union troops in the commonwealth, Federal officials in Washington, and lawmakers in Frankfort and their constituents.

Slaveholding Kentuckians and members of the state's General Assembly generally opposed the Emancipation Proclamation. It inspired slaves to flee to Federal lines where Union officers tended to ignore the distinction between whether a slaveholder was a loyalist or pro-Confederate.[29] In 1864 the wife of a Kentuckian who served as an officer in the USCT wrote Lincoln, informing him of the preponderance of Rebel sympathizers in the state and the power of slavery. "It is something like bearding the lion in his den," Carrie H. Purnell told the president, "with the comfortable assurances that roar as he will—His voice is his only weapon." She added: "Thank God—the day is gone by forever when death or a penalty worse than death was the fate of those who dared to say a black man had a soul."[30]

In mid-1863, when the War Department took a census for the possible draft of Kentucky's 4,130 free black males, Generals Jeremiah T. Boyle and Ambrose E. Burnside warned Lincoln that the state's whites considered drafting blacks a revolutionary step, that slaveholders would violently resist enlistment of their slaves, and that arming blacks would possibly drive away white enlistees. They recommended that Lincoln exempt the commonwealth from the military enrollment and that black men continue to serve as laborers. On July 22 Stanton accepted these recommendations, temporarily suspending the military enrollment of black Kentuckians but, on the president's initiative, stepping up recruitment of blacks freed by the Emancipation Proclamation along the Mississippi River.[31]

That fall, Kentucky's new governor, Thomas E. Bramlette, informed the president that he deeply feared black recruitment in his state, what he termed "the dire effects of such a movement upon the interests of my people."[32] Lincoln calmed Bramlette, at least for a time, informing him that Kentucky slaves would not be recruited, though enlistments of black men would commence in the other border states. Lincoln continued to give Kentucky special status, according to Stanton, because so many of its bondsmen already had been impressed as military laborers. Bramlette expressed alarm, however, in December, when word reached him that a Federal officer, Captain Edward Cahill, had been recruiting Kentucky free blacks to meet the state's draft quota.[33]

In January the War Department began enlisting blacks for a black artillery regiment in Paducah, in the military Department of the Tennessee. Kentucky's 40,285 slaves of draft age apparently proved too attractive to Federal recruiters determined to fill draft quotas. Out-of-state recruiting agents noticed too, descending on the state, looking to fill regiments.[34] The Paducah recruiting project outraged Bramlette, who protested loudly to Lincoln, arguing that Kentucky had met its draft quota with white enlistees, and that military recruiters were violating Kentucky law. The governor warned that if the military did not halt its actions, his government would array "the civil powers of the State" against Federal officers. Bramlette's threat, according to one historian, was analogous to "nullification."[35]

Though Adjutant General Thomas shut down the Paducah recruiting post temporarily, matters between Lincoln and Bramlette deteriorated further. In February the Federal government increased its call for troops to five hundred thousand men and passed an Enrollment Act opening recruitment to "all able-bodied male colored persons, between the ages of twenty-and forty-five years." Loyal slaveholders were to be compensated $300 in lieu of the bondsman's future service, and the slaves were to receive their freedom. On February 29 Provost Marshal General Fry ordered the enrollment "of all colored males of military age," thereby opening the floodgates for Federal recruiters and northern recruiting agents to fill their conscription quotas in the commonwealth. Soon an average of one hundred black men per day were enlisting at Louisville's Taylor Barracks.[36]

On March 8 Bramlette wrote Lincoln a harsh letter, accusing him of breaking his word by recruiting blacks in Kentucky. The governor informed Lincoln that "Kentuckians will obey willingly any law requiring their services in defence of their Government . . . but they will not obey a law violative of their Constitutional rights as Citizens, which dishonors them by preferring the slave to the loyal Kentuckian and which takes private property for public use without just compensation, and without any necessity or excuse. Such law can only by enforced by a hard and dangerous constraint." The governor explained that Kentuckians would sacrifice everything for principle, "*but principle for nothing*," and implored Lincoln "to withold this cup of bitterness and humiliation from the loyal lips of Kentucky." Bramlette next threatened Lincoln: "Do not sow to the winds—least you reap the whirlwind."[37] Four days later the governor wired the provost marshal in Boyle County: "If the president does not, upon my demand, stop the negro enrollment, I will."[38]

The following day J. A. Jacobs of Danville, Kentucky, apprised Lincoln that no subject threatened good relations between Kentucky and the Federal government, and between Kentuckians and the chief executive, as seriously as the enlistment of black soldiers. "It is eminently distasteful and obnoxious to the largest portion of the loyal people of the State," Jacobs wrote, "and there is no small danger of its producing an outbreak of a portion of our loyal people, and I dreadfully fear a conflict between the federal and State authorities."[39]

Bramlette worried that the furor over Lincoln's black recruitment policies would foment so much dissent that his state might go over to the Rebels. Though he preferred instituting "legislative nullification" if Lincoln failed to halt military enrollments, Bramlette ultimately settled on a more moderate path. On March 15 he appealed to Kentuckians to accept military enrollments of black men, which, after all, only determined the names of those eligible for possible military service and did not initiate actual enlistment. The governor urged Kentuckians to resist Lincoln's emancipation program through the ballot box, not through "crimes of violence" or "unlawful resistance."[40]

Furious with Lincoln's policies, on March 26 Bramlette, along with editor Albert G. Hodges of the *Frankfort Commonwealth* and former senator Archibald Dixon, met with the president in Washington to voice their displeasure. They objected to recruiting agents' interference with slaves and to what they considered the government's incorrect calculation of Kentucky's draft quota. The Kentucky delegation seemed mollified by Lincoln's response, agreeing that the commonwealth's draft quota would be adjusted, that the government would recruit Kentucky's blacks only when the state's whites failed to meet its quota, and that if such recruitment occurred, it would proceed legally "&, as far as practicable, free from collateral embarrassments, disorders & provocations."[41] Lincoln responded in his famous April 2 public letter to Hodges, in which the president reiterated his longstanding distaste for slavery, his frustration over wartime emancipation, his rationale for recruiting African Americans, and prefiguring his second inaugural address, his hope that Divine intervention would end the "great wrong" of slavery.[42]

Unfortunately for conservative Kentuckians, the rapprochement between Bramlette and Lincoln lasted only briefly. When, in April, Kentucky failed to meet its recruitment quotas with whites, General Stephen G. Burbridge, the new commander of the District of Kentucky, started recruiting slaves regardless of their masters' loyalty or whether or not the black men wished to enlist. Soldiers summarily arrested those who interfered with the recruitment of slaves. As a result, bondsmen quickly inundated recruiting posts in Covington, Louisville, Owensboro, and Paducah. A Kentucky unit of the USCT, the 120th, rounded up every black male it could find in Henderson and Union Counties.[43] General Augustus L. Chetlain explained how his men went about "forcing able bodied colored men into the Union ranks." "A company of colored troops, fully equipped, would be sent to a certain section of the state, with orders to bring in all colored men found of suitable age and of apparent good health and physique," he said. "After an examination by an army surgeon, all the rejected were sent back to their homes. The owners of those accepted as fit for service had a receipt given to them with the proviso inserted that all owners would when the time came be paid by the government, $300, for each slave, provided they proved their loyalty to it."[44]

Within weeks reports reached Lincoln that Burbridge's recruiters were employing press-gang techniques—"seizing negroes and carrying them off without their consent, and according to no rules whatever, except those of absolute violence"—in northwestern Kentucky. Accordingly, the president ordered Adjutant General Thomas to report back to him "and see that the making soldiers of negroes is done according to the rules you are acting upon, so that unnecessary provocation and irratation be avoided."[45] About eight months later, complaints again surfaced from around Henderson, Kentucky, that Federal officers were coercing slaves to join the USCT. Lieutenant Colonel John Glenn of the 120th USCT reportedly was "forcing negroes into the Military service," Lincoln wrote, "even torturing them—riding them on the rails and the like—to extort their consent." The president ordered Glenn not to force black enlistees any more than white recruits.[46] He also ordered Stanton to investigate accusations that recruiting officers in Maysville, Kentucky, were coercing slaves into service.[47] General Thomas confirmed that such excesses existed, and he assured Lincoln that the impressments of Kentucky blacks would cease.[48] In fact, their forcible induction into the army continued until the war's end.

In September Bramlette wrote Lincoln a blistering letter, strongly objecting to what he considered the unfair treatment accorded the commonwealth by the Federal government, its "military follies and harassments," especially the recruitment of slaves of loyal citizens. Bramlette informed Lincoln that though he and other Kentuckians remained loyal, they were equally committed to "preserving the rights and liberties of our own race." He continued: "We are not willing to sacrifice a single life, or imperil the smallest right of free white men for the sake of the negro." The governor, who was either myopic or who simply ignored the social revolution evolving around him, insisted that the status of African Americans, whether as slaves or free men, should play no role in the restoration of the Union.[49]

When, in February 1865, Lincoln asked General John M. Palmer to command the Department of Kentucky, the officer unsuccessfully tried to refuse the assignment, admitting "I do'nt want to go to Kentucky and spend my time quarreling with the politicians." To this Lincoln replied, "Go to Kentucky, keep your temper, do as you please, and I will sustain you."[50] In one of his first official actions, on March 12, 1865, Palmer authorized the emancipation of the wives and children of Kentucky's black soldiers. Congress had legislated this nine days earlier, and the president endorsed it.[51]

As in the other border states, enlistment of black men in Kentucky hastened slavery's deterioration. Fifty-seven percent of the state's black men between the ages of eighteen and forty-five, free and slave, ultimately donned the Union blue, the highest percentage of any state. By war's end almost twenty-four thousand Kentucky African Americans enlisted in the USCT. Only Louisiana had a larger number of men in black units.[52] Slavery did not end in the commonwealth until December 6, 1865, however, when twenty-seven states, but not Kentucky, ratified the Thirteenth Amendment. Kentuckians did not ratify it until more than a century later, on March 18, 1976.

* * *

General Thomas's success in the Mississippi Valley contributed to the growth of northern support for Lincoln's emancipation program. Writing in May 1863, Attorney General Edward Bates noted that "abolition seems be the strongest rallying point" in Washington, "and men who dont care a fig about it, have become all of a sudden, very zealous in that cause." He included among them Secretary of State William H. Seward and Secretary of War Stanton. A month later Whitelaw Reid, columnist for the *Cincinnati Gazette*, commented on the dramatic change in public opinion concerning the recruitment of African American soldiers: "The day for raising a panic over Negro enlistment has passed; and it, like confiscation, emancipation and a dozen other bitterly denounced 'Abolition measures,' has passed as an accepted fact into the history of the war."[53]

Thomas's recruiting efforts also underscored the need for a centralized Federal system of recruitment. In May 1863, the War Department issued General Orders No. 143, establishing the USCT in regiments to "be numbered *seriatim*, in the order in which they are raised."[54] This order standardized the recruitment process by establishing a separate office in the adjutant general's office, the Bureau of Colored Troops (BCT), to coordinate the organization of black troops. Unlike white soldiers, who served largely in state units, the USCT were Federal soldiers.[55] Led by Assistant Adjutant General Charles W. Foster, the BCT moved quickly to appoint Federal recruiters, authorize recruiting stations, supervise enlistments, and examine officer candidates for regiments that, by the summer 1863, were assigned numbered units in the USCT.[56] With the exception of a few black regiments formed in Connecticut, Louisiana, and Massachusetts (including the Fifty-Fourth and Fifty-Fifth Massachusetts Volunteer Regiments and the Fifth Massachusetts Cavalry)—all other African American units, including those previously mustered on the state level, entered Federal service and eventually received numbered U.S. regimental designations.

For example, under Federal auspices Colonel Thomas Wentworth Higginson's First South Carolina Volunteers became the Thirty-Third

USCT, General James H. Lane's First Kansas Colored Volunteers became the Seventy-Ninth USCT, General Benjamin F. Butler's First, Second, and Third Louisiana Native Guards became, respectively, the Seventy-Third, Seventy-Fourth, and Seventy-Fifth USCT, and the First Arkansas Volunteers of African Descent became the Forty-Sixth USCT. No longer were African American troops enlisting to fight for particular states, but rather for the national government that had freed the slaves. Significantly, federalizing the African American volunteers elevated the USCT from "its original amateurish, haphazard, and volunteer basis to a new footing of professional, organized, regularized activity under central control from Washington."[57]

The mobilization of black troops would have failed, however, had African Americans not enthusiastically encouraged their sons, brothers, and husbands to enlist. Meeting, for example, at a black state convention in Poughkeepsie, New York, in July 1863, "the Colored Citizens of the State of New York" declared "that men of negro lineage hold the balance of power in this contest, and . . . we should . . . throw our weight for the Government, not alone in words, but by sturdy blows. We should strike, and strike hard, to win a place in history, not as vassals, but as men and heroes."[58] That month Frederick Douglass, drawing upon the powerful symbols of armed and uniformed blacks, once again spurred his brethren to enlist. As he explained in now-famous words, "Once let the black man get upon his person the brass letters U.S.; let him get an eagle on his button, and a musket on his shoulder, and bullets in his pocket, and there is no power on earth or under the earth which can deny that he has earned the right of citizenship in the United States."[59]

Though Douglass never joined the USCT (Stanton promised him a commission as a recruiter of black troops in Mississippi but then reneged on that overture), he actively recruited men for the USCT and gave numerous speeches at recruitment camps. Two of his sons, Charles and Lewis, served in the Fifty-Fourth Massachusetts Volunteers. A third son, Frederick Jr., recruited black troops in Mississippi. In August 1864 Lincoln called Douglass to the White House proposing that he form a corps of black scouts to go surreptitiously behind Confederate lines to inform the slaves of the president's Emancipation

Proclamation and to encourage them to enter Federal camps. He left his meeting with Lincoln energized—with a newfound belief in the president's deep commitment to emancipation, not just as a "military necessity."[60]

* * *

The men who joined the USCT were a varied lot. According to Colonel Norwood P. Hallowell of the Fifty-Fifth Massachusetts Volunteers, the regiments recruited from the free states "contained every known variety of citizen of African descent, and were recruited from every class and condition of colored society."[61] For example, the soldiers of the Twenty-Eighth USCT, an Indiana regiment, came largely from Maryland and Delaware. Though 77 percent of the enlistees listed their prewar occupations as farmer or laborer, the unit's muster rolls enumerated nineteen other occupations, most notably "unknown" (7.2 percent), barber (3 percent), "other" (2.8 percent), waiter (2.4 percent), cook (1.4 percent), and teamster (1 percent).[62]

Hallowell compiled statistics on his Massachusetts regiment, which he considered typical of units recruited in the North—and his soldiers were indeed a mixed group. Of the 961 enlisted men in the Fifty-Fifth Massachusetts Volunteer Regiment, the largest number (222) were born in Ohio, followed by Pennsylvania (139), Virginia (106), Indiana (97), Kentucky (68), Missouri (66), and Illinois (56). The remaining 207 men were born in eighteen states (including eleven slave states), the District of Columbia, Nova Scotia, Canada, Africa, and "unknown." Collectively the men had plied forty-six trades and occupations. The most common profession was farmer (596), followed by laborer (74), waiter (50), cook (27), teamster (27), sailor (20), mason and plasterer (16), and hostler and shoemaker (9 each). The recruits served in thirty-five other occupations, ranging from broom maker to glass grinder to confectioner. The men included 247 former slaves, 550 "pure blacks," 430 men of "mixed blood," 477 men who were literate, 319 men who could read and write, 52 church members, and 219 married men. The average age of the recruits was twenty-three and one-fifth years, and their average height was five feet, seven-twelfths of a foot. The men had one thing decidedly in common, Hallowell reported. They entered camp uniformly "poor and ragged."[63]

Once mustered into service, officers employed two methods to training the recruits. In regiments such as the Fifty-Fourth and Fifty-Fifth Massachusetts Volunteers, composed largely of free blacks, commanders resorted to the strict discipline commonly used in drilling whites. "The unruly members of the Fifty-fourth and Fifty-fifth were stood on barrels, bucked, gagged and, if need be, shot; in fact, treated as white soldiers were in all well-disciplined regiments." In contrast, Higginson's First South Carolina Volunteers were former slaves, and he used a more "enlightened" method to train them. "In a slave regiment," Hallowell explained, "the harsher forms of punishment were, or ought to have been, unknown, so that every suggestion of slavery might be avoided." Hallowell believed that whether free black or slave, once the recruit received his new uniform he became a new man. "He straightened up, grew inches taller, lifted, not shuffled, his feet, began at once to try, and to try hard, to take the position of the soldier." The colonel insisted: "For the first time in his life he found himself respected, and entrusted with duties, for the proper performance of which he would be held to a strict accountability." Under the command of competent white commanders like himself, Hallowell concluded, each black volunteer became "a possible Lord Chesterfield."[64]

Higginson's regiment had a different demographic profile. Virtually every man had been enslaved until just days before their muster into the First South Carolina Volunteers. Most came from plantations on the South Carolina or Georgia Sea Islands or from farms on the adjoining mainland. Company G was exceptional in that it contained a number of men from northeastern Florida. Most of the recruits in Higginson's unit were young—in their late teens or twenties—but men in their thirties, forties, and even older also enlisted in the regiment. Its muster-in forms listed most of the men's previous occupations as laborer. Experts with the hoe and plow, they had cropped the long-staple cotton ubiquitous on the Carolina and Georgia Sea Islands. The occupations listed by the former slaves, now Union soldiers, also included house servant and such artisans as carpenter, cooper, mason, and shoemaker.[65]

* * *

Though many abolitionists, northern free blacks, and USCT recruits assumed that African Americans would serve as officers in USCT regiments, white soldiers, U.S. government officials, and white civilians generally frowned upon elevating blacks to the status of commissioned officers. "The real question," Assistant Adjutant General Foster asked in 1864, was whether "white officers and men [were] prepared to acknowledge and obey the colored man, or officer, as a military superior?" Mirroring contemporary white supremacist views, War Department officials answered negatively, arguing that black officers would prove untenable if circumstances placed them in command of whites. Blacks and their white allies objected to color determining rank and bombarded Washington with demands for the commissioning of capable black soldiers.[66]

Nevertheless Lincoln commissioned fewer than one hundred black officers in the USCT. Roughly two-thirds of these men served early in the war in the Louisiana Native Guards until General Nathaniel P. Banks, General Benjamin F. Butler's successor as commander of the Department of the Gulf, forced them to resign their commissions. The remaining handful of African American officers served as company-level officers, chaplains, surgeons and, late in the war, as recruiters. None held field or line command. Blacks who held even these non-command positions encountered racism at every turn. In 1864, for example, six white surgeons wrote Lincoln, complaining that Dr. Alexander T. Augusta, a black surgeon commissioned a major, commanded them at Maryland's Camp Stanton. Despite Augusta's rank and seniority, they refused to serve under him. Augusta was reassigned.[67] That year the Reverend Henry M. Turner, chaplain of the First USCT, while traveling on an inland steamer in Virginia, was forced to dine in Jim Crow facilities and pay an exorbitant fare for inferior quality food. When Turner complained, he suffered harassment and threats from the boat's chief steward.[68]

Thousands of black soldiers, however, served ably as noncommissioned officers at the regimental (sergeant-major, quartermaster sergeant, commissary sergeant, hospital steward) and company (first sergeant, sergeant, and corporal) levels. These men provided leadership and became vital intermediaries between white officers and black enlisted men without revolutionizing American race relations. Near the war's end, the black abolitionist and African explorer Dr. Martin R. Delany urged Lincoln both to commission black officers and to take steps to alleviate what he termed "the heartless and almost relentless prejudice exhibited towards the blacks by the Union army."[69] Lincoln arranged for Delany to receive a commission as a major of infantry, but he served as a recruiter on detached duty, not as a line officer, and served later in the Freedmen's Bureau.

In May 1863 the BCT instituted boards for rigorous examinations of prospective white USCT officers. Service as an officer with the USCT appealed to a broad range of whites—abolitionists and "careerists," paternalists and racists, many of whom rushed to take the examination to lead black regiments. Determined to weed out weak applicants, Lincoln's government made the examination competitive. Only 560 of the first 1,051 men to stand for the test passed.[70] Abolitionist officers included men such as Colonels Higginson and Robert G. Shaw of the Fifty-Fourth Massachusetts Volunteers, and Nathan W. Daniels, commander of the Second Louisiana Native Guard (Union). Reflecting on the qualities of his men and his service in March 1863, Daniels identified "many rough diamonds among this race" and remarked "what they need is only cultivation and opportunity. The Bonds of a half dozen centuries could not smother their inherent capacity." Grateful for the opportunity to lead black men in combat, Daniels added: "Thank God it hath been my fortune to be a participator in the grand idea of proclaiming freedom to this much abused & tortured race. Thank God my Regiment an African one."[71]

Careerist officers were those soldiers eager to take advantage of the War Department's policy of offering promotions to men willing to leave their white regiments to serve in black units. They sought the higher pay, perquisites, and prestige accorded commissioned officers. The examining boards were a mixed lot. Some had decidedly high standards, others were incredibly lax. By war's end about 60 percent of the almost four thousand men who stood for the examination for original commissions or promotions passed. Ultimately, only

25 percent of the applicants received USCT commissions. In many cases, the USCT's officer selection system by competitive examination guaranteed black regiments higher quality leadership than that provided white regiments.[72]

Many of the approximately seven thousand white officers assigned to USCT regiments took advantage of the opportunity to gain in rank by serving with the USCT, advancing from private or sergeant to lieutenant, or from captain to colonel. The promotion of battle-tested noncommissioned and junior officers from white to black units (almost 80 percent of the white officers had prior combat experience) provided the USCT with a generally strong officer corps. For instance, Sergeant Charles Trowbridge of the First New York Engineers gained promotion to captain in the First South Carolina Volunteers. He eventually commanded the regiment.[73]

Sam Evans of Brown County, Ohio, jumped at the chance to advance in rank by moving from an all-white unit to a black one. In May 1863 Evans left the Seventieth Ohio Volunteer Infantry as a private to join the newly organized Fifty-Ninth USCT as a lieutenant. Sam's father disapproved, saying that he "would rather clean out S––t houses at ten cents pr day," than assume such "a degraded position." Lacking confidence in blacks, Andrew Evans asked Sam, "What could four white men do with 100 armed negros if they should become mutinous?" Justifying his decision to transfer, Sam explained: "My place is easier than a private, have better quarters and more privileges," including riding a horse. Besides the improved circumstances afforded by his promotion, Evans believed that service with an African American unit would help save white men's lives and carried with it no social opprobrium. He explained: "a Negro is no better than a white man and has just as good a right to fight for his freedom and the government."[74]

Few white officers of the USCT, however, failed to be smirched by the racism of their day. Two days after Lincoln issued the Emancipation Proclamation, Sergeant Jacob Bruner of the Sixty-Eighth Ohio Volunteer Infantry, a white unit, wrote his wife: "For my part I do not care whether they [the slaves] are free or not. . . . [I]f general emancipation takes place they will swarm to the north by the thousands, much to the detriment of poor white laborers. I hold it is the imperative duty of the United States government to send them out of the country and colonize them." Three months later, Bruner reported on Adjutant General Thomas's recruitment efforts in northeastern Louisiana: "Uncle Abe has at last sensibly concluded to arm the darkey and let him fight." Following his commission as a lieutenant in the Ninth Louisiana Regiment of African Descent, Bruner explained: "My wages will be . . . thirteen hundred and twenty six dollars a year! . . . [N]ow my dear what do you think of it[,] did I meet your approbation in accepting?"[75]

DISCRIMINATION FRONT AND REAR

Lincoln's black soldiers faced more serious problems than white officers who were committed more to higher wages than to racial equality. According to historian and former USCT soldier George Washington Williams, the African American soldier "had enemies in his rear and enemies in his front." Aghast at the mistreatment, degradation, and discrimination under which the men of the USCT served, *Cincinnati Gazette* columnist Whitelaw Reid complained that "every Negro we enlist goes into the field with a halter around his neck." The black troops, he said, encountered "tenfold the dangers our white soldiers incur and none of the protections." As he prepared to enter combat in the summer 1863, Corporal James Henry Gooding of the Fifty-Fourth Massachusetts Volunteers summarized the realities of black military service. "There is not a man in the regiment who does not appreciate the difficulties, the dangers, and maybe ignoble death that awaits him, if captured by the foe, and they will die upon the field rather than be hanged like a dog." Seeking relief from Secretary of War Stanton from the "Veary Hard & a Dreadfull condishion," under which his regiment suffered in New Bern, North Carolina, a soldier of the Fourth USCT wrote "that i hope that the Time Shall Soon come when Shall all be Eacklize as men hear." He added: "i have read the Regulations Enough to Know that it is Rong but i Supose that because we are colored that they think that we dont no any Better."[1]

Lincoln's recruiters had indeed promised black enlistees fair and equal treatment. But in practice the color line circumscribed virtually every aspect of black military life, mirroring racial proscriptions for free blacks in the antebellum North. The twin forces of white racism and military necessity converged on the men of the USCT, and throughout their service black soldiers received discriminatory duties, inferior assignments, inadequate care, insufficient training, and insults from white soldiers. Conditions for the USCT were generally separate and unequal to that of white troops—a condition that underscored their second-class status in the War Department's bureaucracy and in American society at large.

From the start of their military service, many white commanders believed that black troops were better suited to labor than to soldier—to perform manual labor and menial duties, not serve in combat. This is not surprising because, when welcoming blacks into "the armed service of the United States" in his final Emancipation Proclamation, Lincoln specifically directed them "to garrison forts, positions, stations, and other places." The president's intent was clear: blacks were "to garrison," freeing up whites "to fight." Convinced that blacks would prove inferior to whites in combat but were well-suited to work under the hot tropical sun and in unhealthy lowlands, white commanders assigned black troops an inordinate amount of fatigue labor, oftentimes replacing white units for these onerous tasks.[2]

In September 1863, Private John H. Westervelt of the First New York Engineer Corps criticized how the black troops were "ill used by those whose duty it is to look after their interest and see them get what Uncle Sam intends to provide for all alike both white and black." Though he denied being "a nigger worshiper," Westervelt nonetheless noted the disproportionate amount of labor that the men of the USCT performed during the siege of Charleston. "They certainly do more fatigue duty, and I believe there is no longer any question about their [sic] being good fighters. They are put at the hardest as well as the meanest kinds of work. I have seen them policing (cleaning up filth and rubbish) white regiment camps. If a spirited white solider were to do this except as punishment for some offense I think he would die first."[3]

Often the men of the USCT seemed to do little more than construct fortifications, dig trenches, and load and unload supply wagons, ships, and trains. "Instead of the musket," Nimrod Rowley, a New Yorker in the Twentieth USCT, informed President Lincoln from Camp Parapet, Louisiana, "It is the spad and the Whelbarrow and the Axe . . . cuting in one of the most horable swamps in Louisiana stinking and misery. . . . Men are Call to go on thes fatiuges wen sum of them are scar Able to get Along." Another infantryman, Thomas D. Freeman of the Fifty-Fourth Massachusetts Volunteers, complained that "we are not Soldiers but Laborers working for Uncle Sam for nothing but our board and clothes . . . it is nothing but work from morning till night Building Batteries Hauling Guns Cleaning Bricks clearing up land for other Regiments to settle on . . . now do you call this Equality if so God help such Equality."[4]

Because of such protests, in General Orders No. 21, issued in June 1864, Adjutant General Thomas instructed commanders to distribute labor and fatigue detail equally among soldiers of both races. Despite Lincoln's special prodding, General William T. Sherman, long doubtful of the fighting qualities of black soldiers, employed them principally as laborers, teamsters, and servants. Throughout their military service black troops continued to perform manual and menial labor out of proportion to that allotted whites. Two months after Appomattox, officers of the Fifteenth USCT still complained of the excessive garrison and fatigue duty assigned their men.[5]

Such onerous work details, especially in isolated unhealthy posts, and receiving generally insufficient and inferior regimental medical care, contributed to black soldiers' suffering from significantly higher morbidity and mortality rates than whites. Though more than one-third (68,178) of the black soldiers who served in the army died, only 2,751 perished in action. The rest either were reported missing or died from wounds or disease. Approximately one in five black soldiers succumbed to disease as compared to roughly one of every twelve white soldiers. Often while serving as garrison troops, the USCT frequently yielded to diseases common to troops confined in locations with impure water and subjected to deadly infectious organisms. Their dreadful, inferior medical care resulted in more than twenty-nine thousand USCT dying from such diseases as pneumonia, dysentery, typhoid fever, and malaria. "Very few surgeons will do precisely the same for blacks as they would for whites," remarked a surgeon assigned to a USCT regiment in 1863. Roughly 13.5 percent of white soldiers died during the war, while the rate for the USCT was 18.5 percent. Though African American troops experienced considerably less combat than whites, they died at far higher rates.[6]

Because Lincoln's military administrators generally considered black troops inferior to whites, and because the War Department initially defined blacks primarily as military laborers, not soldiers, African American units commonly received inadequate war materiel, rations, and weapons. Engaged in fatigue and garrison work, their uniforms naturally wore out quickly. The Fifth USCT, a regiment of black Ohioans, was a typical unit. It endured insufficient clothing and equipage and deficient housing, forcing its commander, Lieutenant Colonel Giles W. Shurtleff, to improvise. Though the men of the USCT reportedly received the regular army ration provided white troops, the daily allotment of beef and starches catered more to the dietary preferences of white and black northerners than to black southerners. Union Army fare contrasted sharply with the standard diet of slaves, which had included pork, cornbread, and green vegetables. In addition to complaining about their military diet, black troops also faulted the quantity and quality of their chow. Private Westervelt remarked that the blacks routinely congregated "around our cookhouse to get what bean or pea soup we leave. It is allowed in plentifull [sic] quantities by government and goes begging with us, but they receive it with eagerness and swallow it with voracity. Bread is served them only once a week they tell me." And in the case of at least one regiment—the Sixth USCT—a supervisory committee investigated charges that the men received adulterated hardtack.[7]

Lincoln's government armed its USCT regiments with weapons it considered appropriate for the soldiers' military responsibilities. This commonly translated into second- and third-class arms, including the .54 caliber M1855 Austrian "Lorenz" rifled musket, the .69 caliber Austrian rifled musket, and the .69 caliber Prussian musket. Commenting on a failed mission by a black regiment, Colonel Norwood P. Hallowell reported that it fought "with nearly worthless old Austrian rifles, [that were] soon after condemned." To compound problems with their outdated and malfunctioning weapons, some regiments received not only different types of muskets but ones that fired different calibers of ammunition. In April 1864, General Edward W. Hinks requested that troops in his all-black division receive "as effective a weapon as any that are placed in the hands of white Soldiers, who go into battle with none of the peculiar disadvantages to which my men will be Subject." Specifically, Hinks wanted the black soldiers' "unreliable" Springfield and Enfield rifles and "Old Harpers Ferry smoothbore" muskets replaced with Spencer repeating carbines or breech-loading rifles. After the slaughter of approximately two hundred black soldiers at Fort Pillow, Tennessee, on April 12, 1864, he implored General Benjamin F. Butler to equip the men of the Army of the James "to defend themselves and lessen their liability to capture." Because African American troops "cannot afford to be beaten, and will not be taken [prisoner]," Hinks added, they deserved "the best arm . . . that the country can afford." As late as January 1865, a major in the 117th USCT reported that his men had been issued "poor Enfields, but we are making an effort to change them for Springfields."[8]

Black soldiers and their white officers worried about their fate if captured by the Rebels long before the Fort Pillow atrocity, where Confederate General Nathan Bedford Forrest's cavalry massacred 66 percent of the black troops assigned to that Mississippi River garrison. In 1887 Joseph T. Wilson recalled that when he and his black comrades "heard the long roll beat to arms, and the bugle sound the charge, that they were not to go forth to meet those who regarded them as opponents in arms, but who met them as a man in his last desperate effort for life would meet demons." Early in the war Confederate officers announced that slaves convicted of aiding the enemy would be executed—the punishment meted out to southern slaves convicted of insurrection. As soon as Lincoln announced his plan to enlist blacks in Federal military units, Confederates threatened to reenslave them and treat their white officers as inciters of slave rebellion. Armed black men posed "a powerful political symbol in the Confederacy," conjuring up white southerners' worst fears of miscegenation, slave uprising, arson, murder, rape, and pillaging.[9]

If captured the black men who served in Colonel James M. Williams's First Kansas Colored Volunteers faced possible sale as slaves or execution. In May 1863 a large party of Confederate guerrillas massacred a foraging party of black and white Union troops under Williams's command assigned to Indian Territory. Wounded men had "their brains beaten out with clubs, the bloody weapons being left beside them." According to Lieutenant Colonel John Bowles, Confederates in the Trans-Mississippi considered the USCT escaped slaves and their officers instigators of slave insurrection, both subject to immediate execution if captured. Accordingly, Bowles and his men saw no third alternative to fighting or dying, in Bowles's terms, "no branching roads ahead leading to prison or hospital—only one highway, which led to *Victory*—or *Death*." Ironically, during the July 17, 1863, battle of Honey Springs, the largest engagement of the war in Indian Territory, Texas Confederates commanded by General Douglas H. Cooper hesitated to surrender to the black troops, fearing reprisals because of their own executions of black prisoners of war. One of the leaders of the Texas Battalion pleaded with the Union commander General James G. Blunt, "If you'll send white men to take us, we'll surrender, but never to a nigger."[10]

Confederates reacted with outrage to the early efforts to recruit slaves by General David Hunter in South Carolina and Generals John W. Phelps and Butler in Louisiana. In August 1862, the Rebels' Adjutant and Inspector General Samuel Cooper declared Hunter and Phelps "outlaws." When, in November 1862, Confederate troops captured six black soldiers on Georgia's St. Catherines Island, the local commander recommended "that these negroes be made an example of. They are slaves taken with arms in hand against their masters and wearing the abolition uniform. Some swift and terrible punishment should be inflicted that their fellows may be deterred from following their example." Secretary of War James A. Seddon concurred, recommending that one of the blacks "be executed as an example."[11]

Confederate president Jefferson Davis reserved a special animus for Butler and his officers, declaring them "robbers and criminals deserving death." He condemned Butler for exciting "the African slaves . . . to insurrection" and for arming them "for a servile war—a war in its nature far exceeding in horrors the most merciless atrocities of the savages." Davis damned Lincoln's preliminary Emancipation Proclamation as an "effort to excite servile war within the Confederacy" and blasted the final Emancipation Proclamation as "the most execrable measure recorded in the history of guilty man," one that would lead to insurrection by the slaves and to their ultimate "extermination." Captured armed slaves and their white officers would be tried under the laws of the various southern states, he said. Within weeks Methodist preacher George Richard Browder, a Kentucky slaveholder and southern sympathizer, recorded in his diary that "confederates hang or shoot all the negroes they find in uniform & say they will give all the officers captured since the issuing of Lincolns proclamation into the hands of the State authorities to be punished for exciting insurrection. The penalty is death & this may lead to cruel & bloody retaliation. Oh the horrors of these evil times."[12]

By the spring 1863, as Lincoln's program of freeing and arming the slaves unfolded, circumstances led both Confederate and Union leaders to focus on the legal and military status of black U.S. troops. In April, Seddon authorized General John C. Pemberton, commander of the Department of Mississippi and East Louisiana, to put to labor, as he saw fit, an African American, presumably a soldier, captured on a Federal ship. "The Department," Seddon wrote, "has determined that negroes captured will not be regarded as prisoners of war." A month later, in a joint resolution, the Confederate Congress declared that those engaged in freeing and arming the South's slaves would be "lawfully repressed by retaliation." Any white officer of black troops would be considered an insurrectionist, "and shall if captured be put to death or be otherwise punished at the discretion of the court." Captured black soldiers were to "be delivered to the authorities of the State or States in which they shall be captured to be dealt with according to the present or future law of such State or States."[13]

In June, General Edmund Kirby Smith, commander of the Trans-Mississippi Department, discouraged his subordinates from capturing black soldiers or their officers, suggesting instead that they give them "no quarter." The Confederate War Department, however, overruled Kirby Smith's order, describing the men of the USCT as "deluded victims" who "should be received and treated with mercy and returned to their owners. A few examples might perhaps be made," an official explained, "but to refuse them quarter would only make them, against their tendencies, fight desperately." Captured black troops thus faced several possible scenarios. Northern free blacks might be sold into slavery, former slaves might be reenslaved and returned to their masters, or the black soldiers might be executed. Their officers might be executed or imprisoned. Or they all might be forced to perform hard labor.[14]

Mindful of Confederate threats to enslave or execute black soldiers and to execute their officers, in April 1863, Lincoln commissioned Columbia College law professor Francis Lieber to draft what became the first modern code of wartime conduct: General Orders No. 100, issued by the War Department on April 24, 1863. Before large numbers of African Americans troops entered combat, Lincoln sought to establish the principle that his government stood committed to protecting all persons duly admitted into the military service, irrespective of race. By sustaining the doctrine of military necessity, the lawfulness of emancipation, and the equal treatment of black soldiers, "Lincoln's Code," according to one scholar, "integrated the concept of justice into a body of law that had been designed to set justice aside for the sake of humanity."[15]

General Orders No. 100 stated clearly that Lincoln's government expected that its black soldiers and their white officers would be respected as soldiers and, if captured, treated as prisoners of war. Slaves entering Union lines immediately became free. Once black men became soldiers, if captured they were to be treated by their foe as "public enemies," not as individuals. And because international law drew no color distinctions between soldiers, the enslavement or sale of captured men based on race warranted "the severest retaliation, if not redressed upon complaint." The order explained that because the U.S. government could not "retaliate by enslavement; therefore death must be the retaliation for this crime against the law of nations." Legalistic and theoretical, General Orders No. 100 was conspicuously vague and unspecific regarding how and when such "retaliation" would be implemented. "It was a fangless order," according to one scholar, "though pleasing to contemplate."[16]

Senator Charles Sumner implored Lincoln to find a more practical means of protecting the black men of the USCT and their white officers. They needed to be assured that the government would defend them "according to the laws of war, & that not one of them shall suffer without a retaliation, which shall be complete & not vindictive but conservative." Sumner believed that such a proclamation would serve several functions: "give encouragement to the army . . . gratify the country, & . . . teach foreign nations the difference between a barbarous foe & the upholder of Human Liberty. Besides, it would be intrinsically an act of justice."[17]

Theodore Hodgkins, a black New Yorker, informed Secretary of War Stanton that unless Lincoln's administration took immediate steps to protect its African American soldiers, "it may as well disband *all its colored troops* for no soldiers who the government will not protect can be depended upon." Hodgkins proposed a draconian act—a "necessary military execution"—to avenge the Confederate murders of U.S. black troops, one that would get the instant attention of the Rebels and give black volunteers "heart and courage to believe in their government." He implored Stanton to gather the same number of Confederate enlisted men and officers as black Union troops who had been killed "and let them be surrounded by two or three regiments of colored troops who may be allowed to open fire upon them in squads of 50 or 100, with howitzers loaded with grape." Only such an act would teach the Confederates "the the U.S. Govt. is not to be trifled with."[18]

Lincoln did not comment publicly on the treatment of the USCT by the Confederates until late July 1863. He did so following allegations that Confederates murdered or enslaved black soldiers after the battles of Port Hudson (May 27), Milliken's Bend (June 7), and Mound Plantation (June 29) in Louisiana, and at Fort Wagner (July 18) in South Carolina. Port Hudson, Milliken's Bend, and Fort Wagner marked the first use of black troops by the U.S. Army in full-scale combat and convinced many skeptics that African American soldiers would fight with distinction. Confederate threats to give black troops and their white officers "no quarter" inspired the men of the USCT to become stubborn fighters. In 1863 Colonel Nathan W. Daniels wrote proudly that the men of the Second Louisiana Native Guard would "fight like bloodhounds, and never surrender. Defeat in our case is worse than Death. Victory the only alternative—my men are well aware of this and will vent themselves accordingly." Evidence suggests that though southern troops probably executed eleven white USCT officers, the Confederate government never systematically carried out its threat to try captured white officers for insurrection. Generally, the Confederates sent captured black soldiers along with whites to prisoner-of-war camps. Black prisoners, however, were "often not accorded quite the same treatment" as whites.[19]

Frederick Douglass expressed rage over the Confederates' threats, considering them part and parcel of the across-the-board second-class status accorded black troops. And he held Lincoln responsible for such discrimination. Not only had the president failed to protect the men of the USCT and their white officers, he denied blacks commissions as officers, paid black soldiers lower wages than whites, and denied black families humanitarian relief generally provided white troops' families. Douglass exploded with anger when he learned of the Confederates' mistreatment of the Fifty-Fourth Massachusetts Volunteers at Fort Wagner. Though in the battle the black soldiers had "vindicated their sponsors, the abolitionists," the regiment paid a heavy price for its valor. Almost half (272) of the six hundred men who attacked the Confederate battery were killed, wounded, or captured. "Think," Douglass admonished abolitionist George L. Stearns, "of its noble and brave officers literally hacked to pieces while many of its rank and file have been sold into a slavery worse than death, and pardon me if I hesitate about . . . raising a fourth Regiment until the President shall give the same protection to them as to white soldiers." "The slaughter of blacks taken as captives," Douglass complained, "seems to affect him as little as the slaughter of beeves for the use of his army."[20]

On July 30 Lincoln finally drafted his "Order of Retaliation," declaring that the government would protect all of its soldiers—irrespective of color—who became prisoners of war. "To sell or enslave any captured person on account of his color and for no offense against the laws of war is a relapse into barbarism and a crime against the civilization of the age," he declared. Lincoln ordered that "for every soldier of the United States killed in violation of the laws of war a rebel soldier shall be executed, and for every one enslaved by the enemy or sold into slavery a rebel soldier shall be placed at hard labor . . . until the other shall be released and receive the treatment due to a prisoner of war." Despite its bravado, the Federal military never enforced the president's threat. For their part, following Lincoln's retaliation order, Confederate officials elected not to try captured men of the USCT as insurrectionists. They dispatched them instead to prison or labor camps or, on occasion, deciding the fate of black prisoners on the battlefield, executing them.[21]

Lincoln's threats notwithstanding, Confederates put captured black soldiers to work in forced labor battalions. And in at least four other engagements in 1864—Fort Pillow (April 12); Poison Spring, Arkansas (April 18); and Petersburg and Saltville, Virginia (July 30 and October 2)—Confederate troops murdered surrendering or wounded black troops. Following the Fort Pillow bloodbath, Lincoln admitted to an audience at a fair in Baltimore that while he was "determined to use the negro as a soldier, there is no way but to give him all the protection given to any other soldier. The difficulty is not in stating the principle," he said, "but in practically applying it."[22]

The experiences of men of the Eighth USCT, captured by the Confederates at the Battle of Olustee (February 20, 1864) and incarcerated at Andersonville—the Confederacy's notorious Georgia prison—typified the treatment accorded black prisoners of war and their white officers. Private Robert Knox Sneden of the Fortieth New York Volunteers observed "a dozen or more Negroes, all prisoners of war" at Andersonville. "Nearly all are minus an arm or leg, and their wounds are yet unhealed. Many of them are gangrened and they will all surely die. They keep by themselves and are very quiet. The Rebels have removed every vestige of any uniform they once wore, and they have nothing on but old cast off jean trousers and cotton shirts. All are bareheaded, barefooted, and as thin as skeletons. Those captured who were able to work are kept at work outside by the Rebels, felling trees, making roads, etc., etc." Their officers had been sent to prisons in Richmond, Sneden added, "and are made to eat and sleep with Negroes."[23]

Though Lincoln had little control over how the Confederates treated black prisoners of war, he ultimately remedied another discrimination black soldiers endured—unequal wages. The discrepancy in pay was the Lincoln administration's most egregious example of refusing to accept black men as equals. The unequal pay question incited the men of the USCT and their supporters for much of the war. For their part, politicians did little to ameliorate the problem, hoping that paying black soldiers less than whites would render the arming of blacks more palatable to northerners. According to one authority, however, "it appeased no one. Whites who opposed black enlistment recognized unequal pay for what it was, a sop."[24]

As early as August 1862, Stanton had promised black recruits the same pay as whites ($13 per month, $3 of which constituted a clothing allowance), but in 1863 War Department solicitor William Whiting ruled that under the Militia Act of July 1862, blacks of all ranks were to be paid $10 per month with $3 withheld by the government for clothing. Framers of the act had assumed—erroneously—that African Americans who joined the army would serve not as soldiers, but as laborers, and, accordingly, should be paid at a lower rate than white soldiers. Stanton confirmed the lower rate of pay for blacks in June 1863. In response to this blatant inequity, the soldiers of the Fifty-Fourth and Fifty-Fifth Massachusetts Volunteers protested, refusing to accept any pay that was unequal pay. "A more pitiful story of broken faith," recalled Captain Luis F. Emilio of the Fifty-Fourth regiment, "with attendant want and misery upon dependent ones, than this . . . cannot be told." "Notwithstanding the negroes fight so well and show so much bravery," Private Wilbur Fisk of the Second Vermont complained, "they have hitherto been allowed but the bare pittance of seven dollars a month."[25]

Lincoln's government further discriminated against black troops in terms of their service commitment and in the bounties that recruits received. In Pennsylvania, for example, black volunteers enlisted for three-year tours; white volunteers, however, could serve in short-term periods. African American recruits received a $10 bounty from the state's bounty fund but none from the Federal government. White volunteers who volunteered for three years' service received bonuses totaling around $300.[26] The First Michigan Colored Infantry (redesignated the 102nd USCT) initially received no bounty upon enlisting. That changed when local officials realized that bounties served as recruitment incentives and that blacks, not whites, could fill the state's draft quotas.[27]

According to Ohio governor David Tod, who resisted black recruitment for much of the first two years of the war, the discrepancy in pay between whites and blacks was grossly unfair. He recommended that Ohio make up the difference in pay, a practice Massachusetts instituted. "The colored soldier," Tod explained in June 1863, "fills the place of a white man—his risks are as great, if not greater. He is credited to the State upon its quota, thus reducing the draft upon white men. He has proved himself to be a good soldier. Put him then upon an equality so far as dollars and cents are concerned."[28]

Abolitionists and the black soldiers themselves protested loudly against the inequality of pay, arguing correctly that not only had blacks performed well in combat but, because of their race, they commonly faced greater risks than white troops. "Colored men have a right not only to ask for equal pay for equal work," Douglass wrote in August 1863, "but that merit, not color, should be the criterion observed by Government in the distribution of places." Writing in the *New Bedford Mercury*, James Henry Gooding of the Fifty-Fourth Massachusetts Volunteers explained why his regiment refused to accept any pay until it was offered equal pay. "Too many of our comrades' bones lie bleaching near the walls of Fort Wagner," he said, "to subtract even one *cent* from our hard earned pay." To accept less, Gooding added, "would rob a whole race of their title to manhood, and, even make them feel, no matter how faithful, how brave they had been, that their mite towards founding liberty on a firm basis was spurned, and made mock of." "Now your Excellency," Gooding explained to Lincoln, "we have done a Soldier's Duty. Why Can't we have a Soldier's pay? . . . Now if the United States exacts uniformity of treatment of her Soldiers from the Insurgents, would it not be well and consistent to set the example herself by paying all her *Soldiers* alike?"[29]

While genuinely sympathetic to the injustice accorded the black soldiers in terms of their unequal pay, Lincoln urged them to remain patient. Douglass explained that in August 1863 the president reminded him that many whites still doubted the wisdom of enlisting blacks, considering the idea of black soldiers offensive. Lincoln interpreted the differential in pay between white and black troops "a necessary concession to smooth the way to their employment at all as soldiers." Reportedly in a patronizing tone, the president informed Douglass that because black men "had larger motives for being soldiers than white men . . . they ought to be willing to enter the service upon any condition." Eventually, Lincoln said, the government would equalize the pay of black and white soldiers. But the men of the USCT would have to wait.[30]

Douglass, however, and African American troops in the ranks lost "patience and faith" with Lincoln. As late as September 1864, the black leader remained dismayed at the government's "treatment of our poor black soldiers—the refusal to pay them anything like equal compensation, though it was promised them when they enlisted; the refusal to insist upon the exchange of colored prisoners, and to retaliate upon rebel prisoners when colored prisoners have been slaughtered in cold blood, although the President has repeatedly promised thus to protect the lives of his colored soldiers." The black soldiers seethed with indignation over their unequal wages and also because Lincoln's government fell short of providing their families humanitarian relief. As a result the wives, parents, and children of thousands of USCT suffered from sickness and endured poverty.[31]

The men of the Fifty-Fourth and Fifty-Fifth Massachusetts Volunteers, insulted by Federal policy, continued to refuse any pay, even the supplement offered by their state legislature to make up the difference between their promised and actual compensation. Writing from Folly Island, South Carolina, seventy-four men of the Fifty-Fifth Massachusetts explained to Lincoln that they were unwilling to accept the unequal Federal pay, even with the state subsidy: "Troops in the general service are not Paid Partly By Government & Partly By State," and they refused to be treated differently than white soldiers. The men insisted that their pay mattered less to them than the principles of fairness and equity, explaining: "we came to fight For Liberty justice & Equality. These are gifts we Prise more Highly than Gold For these We Left our Homes our Familys Friends & Relatives most Dear to take as it ware our Lives in our Hands To Do Battle for God & Liberty[.]"[32]

In June 1864, Colonel Edward N. Hallowell, who replaced Robert G. Shaw as commander of the Fifty-Fourth regiment after the assault on Fort Wagner, reported that his men, having received no pay in almost a year, were nearly mutinous. "I believe them to be entirely right, morally," Hallowell explained, "and yet military necessity has compelled me to shoot two of them." Conditions were worse in the Third South Carolina Volunteers, where, in protest of the government's unequal pay policy, Sergeant William Walker, a former slave with a long record of challenging his white superiors, marched his company to his commanding officer's tent and ordered them to stack their guns. Walker asserted that because the army had failed to uphold its contract with the soldiers, he and his men were released from duty. His superiors disagreed, and the army court-martialed and executed Walker. According to Colonel Higginson, "fear of such tragedies spread a cloud of solicitude over every camp of colored soldiers for more than a year."[33] Outraged by Walker's execution and the unequal pay that motivated the sergeant's mutinous action, on May 13, 1864, Massachusetts governor John A. Andrew wrote Lincoln, denouncing "the Government which found no law *to pay him except as a nondescript or a contraband*, nevertheless found law enough *to shoot him as a soldier.*"[34]

In his December 1863, annual report, Secretary of War Stanton praised the military performance of the USCT and urged Congress to equalize its pay. "There seems to be inequality and injustice" in their wages, Stanton remarked in a gross understatement. "Soldiers of the Union, fighting under its banner, and exposing their lives in battle to uphold the government, colored troops are entitled to enjoy its justice and beneficence." Nevertheless Lincoln and Republicans in Congress continued to move slowly in remedying this injustice, indicative of the considerable opposition they confronted from Democrats and conservative Republicans in equalizing the status of black and white troops. In January 1864, Higginson informed the *New York Tribune* that the government's failure to honor its pledge to the black regiments "inflicted untold suffering . . . impaired discipline . . . relaxed loyalty, and has begun to implant a feeling of sullen distrust in the very regiments whose early career solved the problem of the nation, created a new army, and made peaceful emancipation possible." In April 1864, Attorney General Edward Bates reversed Whiting's interpretation of the Militia Act (laborers *not* soldiers were to receive $10 per month), thereby paving the way for equal pay. However, Lincoln still refused to act.[35]

Some black soldiers complained about their pay directly to the president, underscoring the distress their low wages caused their families. For example, George Washington of the 123rd USCT, stationed at Taylor Barracks in Louisville, wrote Lincoln asking the president for a military discharge so that he could care for his wife and four children, still enslaved in Oldham County, Kentucky, by "a hard master[,] one that loves the South [and] hangs with it." The slave owner, David Sparks, reportedly refused to give Washington's family clothing, telling them to "let old Abe Giv them Close." Several weeks later another African American soldier, Sergeant John Morgan of the Fourteenth Louisiana Corps d'Afrique, wrote to Lincoln on behalf of the other sergeants in his regiment, most of whom had families living in New Orleans, complaining about the negative impact the inequality of pay had on their households. "We have the same feelings for our wives and children at home and we study the welfare of them as much as the white soldiers," Morgan explained. He added that reports from their families confirmed that they lived "in a starving condition" and the men needed to send them more money. In Morgan's words, "we cant seport them on several dollars per month."[36]

In some military theaters black soldiers' families and slave refugees crowded in and around USCT camps seeking rations, shelter, and humanitarian relief. Early in 1865 Dr. Joseph Smith, a Unionist physician and critic of slavery in Danville, Kentucky, wrote Lincoln, underscoring the serious plight of as many as a thousand African American women and children at Camp Nelson, Kentucky. This four-thousand-acre base on the Kentucky River in Jessamine County served as a large recruiting base and training site; eight USCT regiments organized there, amounting to over fifty-four hundred enlistees. It constituted Kentucky's foremost USCT induction center.[37]

Dr. Smith informed Lincoln that the conditions for refugees and family members of USCT were deplorable. Only one hundred women, those employed as cooks and washerwoman, lived "comparatively decent & comfortable." The rest subsisted in the most shameful manner. "Hundreds crowded together in one room. Some ragged, all dirty, filthy & debauched. Many pregnant since they went there— one half or more labouring under venerial diseases—contracted from the soldiers. Nothing to do, improvident, obscene. This is no exaggeration—it had to be seen to be appreciated in all its horrors. And all this too in the name of humanity!" Dr. Smith urged Lincoln to order that officers exclude women and children from USCT camps unless they could be supported adequately. Ironically, he supposed that they would receive better care from their masters than from the army, adding: "Sir, there is no respectable General who would allow white women of such habits to remain in their camps for one day."[38]

Lincoln sympathized with the plight of the USCT, who received unequal pay, as well as that of their families and other black refugees. In August 1863 he had promised Douglass that ultimately the government would equalize the pay black troops and white soldiers received. In his December 1863 report to Lincoln, Secretary of War Stanton recommended that Congress pay all troops the same. Finally, in June 1864, Congress equalized pay for black and white troops but with a major qualification. Soldiers who had been enslaved at the start of the war would receive retroactive pay only to January 1, 1864. Men free at the beginning of hostilities would earn back pay to the date of their enlistment as well as bounties.[39]

Determined to rectify the discrimination against soldiers who had been slaves, Higginson waged a vigorous campaign in the national press, accusing the government of defrauding former slaves who served in the army and for breaking its contract with them. "Any employer," Higginson wrote to the *Tribune*, "following the example of the United States Government, may make with him [the former slave] a written agreement, receive his services, and then withhold the wages. He has no motive to honest industry, or to honesty of any kind. He is virtually a slave, and nothing else, to the end of time." Not until March 3, 1865, did Congress finally grant full retroactive pay to all black soldiers who had been promised equal pay upon mustering into the service. Two months later the War Department authorized bounties for all black recruits—slave and free—who had enlisted after July 18, 1864. Significantly, the statutes that conferred these bounties were among the first Federal laws based on the principle of equal rights regardless of race. But slaves who enlisted before that date never received such a claim. War Department officials considered the slaves' freedom sufficient bounty.[40]

BATTLES, MASSACRES, PARADES

I n 1886 William Todd, who had served in Company B, Seventy-Ninth Regiment, New York State Militia (the "Highlanders"), recalled when and how his unit, consisting mostly of Scots immigrants or men of Scottish descent, first encountered the USCT. In July 1862, when General David Hunter was recruiting and training what became the First South Carolina Volunteers, the Highlanders, then a battle-hardened unit, witnessed the black troops training at Hilton Head Island and were not impressed.

"When we saw the negroes, uniformed and equipped like ourselves—except that their clothing and accoutrements were new and clean, while ours were almost worn out in active service—parading up and down the wharf, doing guard duty," Todd explained, "it was more than some of our hot-headed pro-slavery comrades could witness in silence." Initially the Highlanders directed "vile epithets" at the black troops, restrained only by their officers from engaging with the men of the USCT in fisticuffs. "It is pleasant to record, however, that very few of the regiment thus disgraced themselves, and in a short time after, when the colored troops became a part of Union army in the field, they were welcomed by us all as brothers in arms."[1]

The Highlanders' experience played out in many white Union units. Though most northerners had enlisted in Abraham Lincoln's army to suppress the rebellion, they quickly came to grasp what the president had realized: the Union's restoration and slavery's destruction were inseparable. To be sure, during the war many, probably most, white soldiers remained prejudiced against soldiers of color. Few white northerners had joined the Union army specifically to free the slaves, but their wartime experiences, including observing for the first time and interacting with slaves, convinced Federal troops of slavery's evils. During the first two years of the war, the bondspeople gradually transformed white Yankee volunteers into "emancipation advocates"—men who equated emancipation with redemption of the American Republic from slavery's sin. After 1863 most white Union troops ultimately backed Lincoln's military emancipation project, mindful that both Union victory hinged on emancipation and that freeing the slaves was essential "to make the Union worth saving." Beyond this, the black soldiers' military performance warmed many white troops to the prospect of black enlistments, though they retained elements of their bias against people of color.[2]

The black soldiers' generally strong performance in combat convinced rank-and-file white troops that black men had earned the right to be treated as equals—at least on the battlefield. An officer in a Maine unit reported in the *Bangor Daily Whig and Courier* that the black troops he observed in Louisiana "are composed of smart men, and I believe just as good men to fight as we have. They learn quick, and take pride in doing their duty well."[3] Another soldier, who enlisted as a private in an Illinois regiment, but garnered captain's bars by serving in the Ninth Louisiana Volunteers of African Descent, defended his black comrades. Following an intense battle in June 1863, in which his company experienced numerous casualties, M. M. Miller informed his aunt: "I never more wish to hear the expression, 'the niggers won't fight.' Come with me 100 yards from where I sit, and I can show you the wounds that cover the bodies of 16 as brave, loyal and patriotic soldiers as ever drew bead on a Rebel." Miller added: "They fought and died defending the cause that we revere."[4]

In exchange, then, for the hardships and indignities they endured—reduced pay, inferior medical care, inadequate weapons, inappropriate rations, insufficient training, the prospect of being enslaved or executed if captured, repeated insults from white troops, brutal punishments that smacked of slave discipline, backwater posts—the USCT achieved a creditable military record. The black soldiers carried out various military duties and at times distinguished themselves in combat. In the process they convinced many northerners, even their severest and most racist critics, of their value to the Union cause.[5]

* * *

The language of Lincoln's final Emancipation Proclamation made clear his original intention that blacks would serve as garrison troops. Eight days before issuing the final document, Lincoln informed Senator Charles Sumner of his intention to raise black troops and to employ them to defend the Mississippi River line, thereby freeing white troops to fight in climates allegedly better suited to them.[6] Less than two weeks after issuing his proclamation, the president wrote to General John A. Dix inquiring whether or not Fortress Monroe or the Federal installation at Yorktown, Virginia, might be manned by black soldiers. "The proclamation has been issued," Lincoln explained. "We were not succeeding—at best, were progressing too slowly—without it. Now, that we have it, and bear all the disadvantage of it, (we do bear some in certain quarters) we must also take some benefit from it, if practicable." Lincoln wondered whether the military posts "could not, in whole or in part, be garrisoned by colored troops, leaving the white forces now necessary at those places, to be employed elsewhere."[7] As late as September 1863, the president still envisioned black soldiers as second-tier troops, informing Tennessee's military governor Andrew Johnson of the importance of his recruiting "every man you can, black and white, under arms at the very earliest moment, to guard roads, bridges and trains, allowing all the better trained soldiers to go forward to [General William S.] Rosecrans."[8]

Like Lincoln, many military commanders initially intended the USCT to play only a defensive role in the military, defending garrisons and guarding railroads. Because of the low expectations many racist white officers had for blacks' abilities as soldiers—"I would use Negros as Surplus," General William T. Sherman growled late in the war—the USCT largely garrisoned forts, escorted wagon trains, performed fatigue labor, and safeguarded confiscated plantations and prisoners of war.[9] Such assignments proved more hazardous than might be supposed, however, given the ebb and flow of offensive and defensive lines. "Infantry escorting a wagon train might receive little warning before finding itself heavily engaged with Confederate raiders, as could happen anywhere from Arkansas to Virginia," writes one authority. And despite the president's cautious rhetoric about how best to employ the USCT, by the time he issued his final Emancipation Proclamation in January 1863, black soldiers already had participated in minor engagements with Confederates in Kansas and South Carolina. "As happened often during a war in which federal policy evolved in reaction to events, practices in the field were far in advance of pronouncements from Washington."[10]

Resulting from necessity and circumstance, the USCT ultimately participated in 449 separate military actions, thirty-nine of which were major engagements. The USCT fought well in the spring and summer of 1863, at Port Hudson and Milliken's Bend, Louisiana, and Fort Wagner, South Carolina, proving their value to many doubters. At Milliken's Bend black soldiers in fact rescued white troops. The black soldiers' famous assault at Fort Wagner, where the Fifty-Fourth Massachusetts Volunteers lost one-half of its force, received national press coverage, turning many former critics and skeptics into supporters of Lincoln's military emancipation project. By the end of the year Secretary of War Edwin M. Stanton reported to Lincoln that though many persons questioned whether the freed slaves had sufficient courage and could adjust to military discipline, combat experience proved "how groundless were these apprehensions." Stanton reported, "The slave has proved his manhood, and his capacity as an infantry soldier, at Milliken's Bend, at the assault upon Port Hudson, and the storming of Fort Wagner."[11]

Though some writers have exaggerated or romanticized the fighting prowess of the USCT, embellishing assessments of their combat with notions of heroism, historians generally agree that the men of the USCT fought on a par with white troops. Bell Irvin Wiley, an early student, complained that though contemporary testimony was too biased to allow an objective evaluation of their fighting, he nevertheless concluded "that some Negro soldiers conducted themselves heroically in battle while others skulked and ran; that leadership was a crucial factor in their combat performance . . . that in offensive spurts the showing of Negroes compared favorably with that of whites of comparable background and training." In short, they discharged their duties more or less like all soldiers, irrespective of time, place, or race. Wiley was on less solid footing, however, when he argued "that units recruited in the North were more effective than those composed of recently freed slaves." Neither Wiley nor other writers have unearthed evidence to support a correlation between free or slave status and military performance. Rather, as in all wars, innumerable factors determined how soldiers fought.[12]

This proved especially so in the experiences of the USCT in the far-off Trans-Mississippi West, the military theater so far least studied by scholars. Many of the exigencies of combat experienced by the USCT in campaigns east of the Mississippi River first played out in Kansas and Missouri. More than a year prior to the Fifth-Fourth Massachusetts's attack on Fort Wagner, African Americans troops engaged the enemy at Locust Grove in the Cherokee Nation. Months before their début in the East, a black regiment fought in Missouri, inspiring the enlistment of African Americans in neighboring states. Similarly the military presence of the USCT in Indian Territory served as a magnet for fugitive slaves, who rushed to join their ranks from as far away as Texas. By the war's close, over fifteen thousand blacks had joined the Union army in an area where the total of Federal volunteers numbered between only thirty and fifty thousand.[13]

In some battles the men of the USCT found themselves more or less thrown into combat. In such actions as the assault on the Confederate bastion at Port Hudson, Louisiana (May 27, 1863), and the engagement at New Market Heights, Virginia (September 29, 1864), black troops, according to Noah Andre Trudeau "were deliberately committed to a hopeless task—not for any strategic reason, but solely to test their mettle." Despite terrible odds, however, the black soldiers performed well in both battles, results that whites acknowledged grudgingly.[14]

Having observed the bravery of the First and Third Louisiana Native Guards at the defeat at Port Hudson, a white New Yorker commented: "They charged and re-charged and didn't know what retreat meant. They lost in their two regiments some four hundred men as near as I can learn. This settles the question about niggers not fighting well. They, on the contrary, make splendid soldiers and are as good fighting men as any we have." A Massachusetts soldier agreed with this assessment of the performance of the black troops at Port Hudson. "A race of serfs stepped up to the respect of the world," he wrote with considerable prescience, "and commenced a national existence." Writing to his wife, Union Colonel Benjamin H. Grierson remarked, "the negro regiments fought bravely yesterday . . . there can be no question about the good fighting qualities of negroes hereafter." Following New Market Heights, where fourteen men of the USCT received the Medal of Honor, the Fifth USCT's Lieutenant Joseph J. Scroggs proclaimed that "no man dare hereafter say aught in my presence against the bravery and soldierly qualities of the colored soldiers."[15]

Raw, virtually untrained black troops, mostly former slaves, exhibited similar dash and grit while defending the Union garrison at Milliken's Bend, Louisiana, twenty-five miles above Vicksburg on the Mississippi River, on June 7, 1863. In this engagement three regiments held off a larger force of Confederates in heated hand-to-hand combat. Their performance was especially noteworthy because the black soldiers entered battle poorly prepared and equipped with outmoded Belgian rifles. They nevertheless fought fiercely but suffered devastating losses—35 percent of the black troops were killed or wounded. The Ninth Louisiana Volunteers of African Descent lost almost 45 percent of its men, the highest proportional loss by a unit in a single engagement during the war. Federal brass took note of the black troops' courage and élan. "The bravery of the blacks in the battle at Milliken's Bend," Assistant Secretary of War Charles A. Dana recalled, "completely revolutionized the sentiment of the army with regard to the employment of negro troops." Accompanying General Ulysses S. Grant's army during the Vicksburg campaign, Dana "heard prominent officers who formerly in private had sneered at the idea of the negroes fighting express themselves after that as heartily in favor of it."[16]

Having tasted their first battle in 1863, black troops gained more opportunities to fight in 1864, achieving battlefield success in several major campaigns and in many small engagements. On February 20 three black regiments suffered heavy casualties during the Union army's defeat at the Battle of Olustee, Florida, along the Florida, Atlantic, & Gulf Central Railroad about sixty miles west of Jacksonville. A correspondent who observed the battle reported to the *Liberator*, "The rebels allowed us to penetrate, and then, with ten to our one, cut us off, meaning to 'bag' us." Incredibly the Eighth USCT, inexperienced in deploying and loading its weapons in combat, served as one of the lead Union regiments and bore the brunt of the Confederates' intense enfilading fire. The regiment held its position during the battle for an hour and a half. When the engagement ended, more than three hundred of the Eighth USCT's 554 effectives lay killed or wounded. The First North Carolina Colored Volunteers lost 230 of its approximately six hundred men and the Fifty-Fourth Massachusetts Volunteers, which covered the Union troops' withdrawal, had eighty-six casualties from among its roughly 495 men. To make matters worse, following the battle Confederate troops brazenly murdered as many as fifty black prisoners. A Rebel soldier instructed his wife to "Tell the negroes if they could have seen how the [northern] negroes are treated I think it would cure them of all desire to go." Another Confederate remarked that at Olustee, "our men slayed the Negrows & if it had not been for the officers their would not one of them been spaired."[17]

One of the lowest points in the history of the USCT occurred at Fort Pillow, Tennessee, on April 12, 1864. The fort, positioned on the Mississippi River north of Memphis, consisted of Tennessee Unionists and men of the Sixth U.S. Colored Heavy Artillery and the Second U.S. Colored Light Artillery. Confederate cavalrymen under General Nathan Bedford Forrest encircled and then massacred the outmanned Union garrison, first commanded by Major Lionel F. Booth (who fell early in the battle) and succeeded by Major William F. Bradford. When Bradford refused to surrender, Forrest's men stormed the fort and killed roughly two hundred of the 262 black men assigned to the post, executing and then butchering the men of the USCT who lay wounded or tried to surrender. A southern journalist reported that "the sight of negro soldiers stirred the bosoms of our soldiers with courageous madness." The Fort Pillow disaster "pushed Lincoln to the limit" on the question of retaliation. How would he protect African American soldiers from Confederate war crimes?[18]

Shocked by the Fort Pillow atrocities, Lincoln endorsed a congressional resolution to investigate the incident and reiterated the point he had made in 1863 regarding the mistreatment of African American troops by the Rebels. Speaking at a fair in Baltimore on April 18, before details of the massacre had been confirmed, Lincoln pledged to protect the black troops. "Having determined to use the negro as a soldier, there is no way but to give him all the protection given to any other soldier. . . . It is a mistake to suppose the government is indiffe[re]nt to this matter, or is not doing the best it can in regard to it." "If there has been the massacre," the president continued, "and being so proven, the retribution shall as surely come. It will be a matter of grave consideration in what course to apply the retribution; but in the supposed case, it must come."[19] Congressional investigators soon substantiated that Forrest's cavalrymen had massacred black troops at Fort Pillow. The atrocities included violating the terms of a truce negotiation, torturing and burning captives, burying wounded soldiers alive, and continuing to fight after the Union troops had surrendered and had requested quarter.[20]

In early May Lincoln solicited opinions from his cabinet members as to how to respond to the Fort Pillow slayings. On May 6 each secretary read his opinion on the case. They agreed that the government had a responsibility to protect all of its soldiers, including the men of the USCT. Attorney General Edward Bates, however, cautioned Lincoln against beginning a policy of senseless, immoral, "mutual slaughter." "Retaliation is not mere justice," he wrote. "It is avowedly Revenge; and is wholly unjustifiable, in law and conscience." That said, a few days later Bates remarked that the Confederates' fighting at Fort Pillow exhibited "a cruel barbarity on the part of the enemy, even worse than first reported."[21]

Secretary of the Navy Gideon Welles recommended that if the Rebels refused to punish the officials responsible for the killings, then "rebel officers [should] be taken into close custody and held accountable for the conduct of the War by the Rebels on humane and civilized principles." Welles found troubling the idea of retribution. He explained in his diary, "The idea of retaliation, killing man for man,—which is the popular noisy demand, is barbarous, and I cannot assent to or advise it. . . . The whole subject is beset with difficulties." While Secretary of the Interior John P. Usher agreed with Bates that Lincoln should avoid retaliatory policies, he nonetheless suggested that the government execute an equal number of Confederate captives "who, since the massacre, have been or may hereafter, from time to time, be captured from Forrests [*sic*] Command, designating, in every instance, as far as practicable, officers instead of privates."[22]

Postmaster General Montgomery Blair roundly condemned retaliation, urging Lincoln to occupy the moral high ground. To do otherwise, Blair warned, would reduce his government to the savage level of their enemy. He added: "Their own people are not so lost to all sense of shame and decency as not to be effected by outrages like this." Like Usher, Secretary of War Edwin M. Stanton recommended that Lincoln take Confederate hostages and, if the insurgents failed to surrender those responsible for the murders, take "measures as may . . . be essential for the protection of union soldiers from such savage barbarities as were practiced at Fort Pillow." Salmon P. Chase, secretary of the treasury, urged the president to execute an equal number of high-ranking Confederate officers "for the Slaveholding class, which furnishes such officers, holds very cheap the lives of the nonslaveholding classes which furnish the privates."[23]

Preoccupied with Grant's Wilderness Campaign, Lincoln hesitated to retaliate against Confederate war crimes directed at the USCT. He deliberated, exhibiting considerable forbearance and restraint and premising his response on the principle that "blood can not restore blood, and government should not act for revenge." He then made at best a lukewarm response.[24]

On May 17 Lincoln submitted to Stanton an incomplete draft on the Fort Pillow murders. He demanded that Confederate authorities agree by July 1 to outlaw future massacres and to treat captured black solders "according to the laws of war," including the exchange of captured black troops for Confederates. If the Rebels refused, then the U.S. Army would retaliate ("take such action as may then appear expedient and just"). Stanton never sent this message.[25]

Lincoln's other steps included symbolically ordering General Forrest to appear in U.S. circuit court to respond to charges of treason, refusing to participate in the prisoner-of-war exchange system until the Rebels agreed to exchange USCT prisoners of war, and cutting rations of Confederates in northern prisons. In the end Lincoln doubtless sought to avoid exacerbating hatred toward the Confederates, creating "a cycle of retaliation," and possibly worsening the treatment of white and black Union soldiers in Rebel prisons.[26] He firmly believed that the best mode of avenging the Fort Pillow killings was in crushing the insurgents and destroying slavery.

Two days after preparing his draft response on Fort Pillow, Lincoln met at the White House with Mrs. Mary Elizabeth Wayt Booth, the widow of the slain commander at Fort Pillow, Major Lionel F. Booth. Writing to Senator Charles Sumner, Lincoln explained that Mrs. Booth "makes a point, which I think very worthy of consideration which is, widows and children *in fact*, of colored soldiers who fall in our service, be placed in law, the same as if their marriages were legal, so that they can have the benefit of the provisions made the widows & orphans of white soldiers." Mrs. Booth and President Lincoln's concern for widows and orphans of deceased black soldiers raised an essential problem that plagued the men of the USCT.[27]

The marriages of those recruits who had been slaves lacked legal sanction because southern states' slave codes never recognized marriages between enslaved men and women. Following up Lincoln's request, Sumner proposed an amendment, reported as a joint resolution by Massachusetts senator Henry Wilson, to an army appropriation bill to provide equal pay for the USCT. The bill gained approval on June 14, 1864. Mrs. Booth, no doubt through Sumner, also influenced the Senate Committee on Pensions to include an amendment to a House bill to provide pensions for widows and children of men of the USCT who died in battle or from disease while in military service. Thanks to Connecticut senator Lafayette S. Foster, this came to pass on July 2, 1864, though Congress restricted the pensions to widows and children only of those soldiers who were free, not slaves.[28]

The Fort Pillow massacre remained a rallying cry for African Americans, especially for the men of the USCT, for the remainder of the war. On June 15, 1864, black troops cried "Remember Fort Pillow" when assaulting the outer defenses of the Confederate stronghold at Petersburg, Virginia. The Third Division, Eighteenth Corps, led by General Edward W. Hinks, stormed the fortified Dimmock Line that circled Petersburg south of the Appomattox River. Despite heavy casualties (almost half of the men of the Fourth USCT were hit), the black troops successfully rushed the twenty-foot-thick breastworks and trenches protected by fifteen-foot ditches. They captured six Confederate batteries, including nine artillery pieces, and took two hundred prisoners. Private Charles Torrey Beman of the Fifth Massachusetts Cavalry remembered how "the shell, grape and canister came around us cruelly," but "we rallied, and after a terrible charge, amidst pieces of barbarous iron, solid shot and shell, we drove the desperate greybacks from their fortifications, and gave three cheers for our victory." "It was rather interesting to see the old veterans of the A[rmy of the] P[otomac] stare when they saw the works we had captured," wrote Lieutenant Harvey Covell of the Sixth USCT.[29]

Convinced that Rebel reinforcements were en route, and still skeptical of the "experiment" of employing black soldiers, Hinks's superior, General William F. Smith, failed to use the USCT to pursue the enemy and missed a perfect opportunity to capture Petersburg. "There was nothing—not even a military force," an exasperated Grant later complained, "to prevent our walking in and taking possession."[30] Attorney General Bates interpreted the USCT's performance at Petersburg differently. To his mind the Petersburg operation illustrated that the blacks would "*charge* as bravely as any troops; but once repulsed and broken, they cant be rallied; because they have no habit of moral discipline."[31] Smith's inaction necessitated the ten-month-long siege of Petersburg.

Despite Smith's indecision and Bates's doubts about blacks as soldiers, the men of the USCT nonetheless proved their worth at the Petersburg assault. Hinks's division experienced its first real combat there, handling itself adequately during its baptism of fire. Summarizing their contribution to the early Petersburg campaign, Private

Wilbur Fisk of the Second Vermont Volunteers wrote, "The negroes were remarkably well pleased with their prowess on this occasion. It was a glorious day for them. They won great favor in the eyes of the white soldiers by their courage and bravery. I am sure I never looked upon negroes with more respect that I did upon those soldiers, and I did not hear a word of disrespect towards them from any of the boys." Commenting on another action by the USCT, Fisk observed: "Yesterday they made another charge here, and it was done in excellent style. The best military critic could hardly find fault with it. In a steady straight line they advanced right over the crest of the hill and right up to the enemy's works, under a terrible fire, but without wavering or faltering, compelling the enemy to leave his works in the hands of the blacks. The stream of wounded that came pouring back, some leaning on a comrade and some carried on stretchers, told of the bloody work they had done."[32] The Reverend William H. Hunter, the black chaplain of the Fourth USCT, interpreted the success of the African American troops at Petersburg in millennial terms. "The 15th of June, 1864," he wrote, "is a day long to be remembered by the entire colored race on this continent. It is the day when prejudice died in the entire Army of the U.S. of America. It is the day when it was admitted that colored men were equal to the severest ordeal. It is the day in which was secured to us the rights of equality in the Army and service of the Government of the United States."[33]

Not only did the Reverend Hunter speak too optimistically about the acceptance and success of blacks in the Federal forces, but six weeks later the USCT participated in one of the Union army's most famous debacles—the bloody assault at the Crater at Petersburg on July 30, 1864. Determined to find a means of penetrating the Dimmock Line and ending the Petersburg siege, General Ambrose Burnside, commander of the Ninth Corps, authorized coal miners from the Forty-Eighth Pennsylvania Volunteers to tunnel 551 feet to the Confederate line, to pack 320 kegs of gunpowder—eight thousand pounds—under the Confederate redoubt known as Elliott's Salient, and to detonate the massive charge. Burnside selected nine well-rested but inexperienced USCT regiments from the Fourth Division, commanded by General Edward Ferrero, to lead the attack after the explosion and to capture Cemetery Hill behind the Confederate lines. These regiments had heretofore been employed for guard detail and fatigue duty, not combat. To prepare them for the attack, the USCT regiments received two weeks of special tactical training that would enable them to quickly circumvent the cavity that would result following the explosion set for July 30. "In conception," one authority explains, the plan "bid fair to become the most brilliant stroke of the war; in execution it became a tragic fiasco."[34]

The explosion and accompanying surge seemed doomed from the start. Less than twenty-four hours before the scheduled blast, Burnside's superiors, Generals George G. Meade and Grant, overruled the decision to have Ferrero's black division spearhead the attack. Like most high-ranking Union officers, Meade and Grant were unsure of the fighting ability of black soldiers. They also feared that should the operation fail, critics would accuse them of recklessly sacrificing African American lives. Accordingly, instead of Ferrero's black troops, three divisions of white soldiers (commanded by Generals James H. Ledlie, Robert B. Potter, and Orlando B. Willcox) prepared to deploy around the periphery of the pit that would result from the detonation of the mine and then capture Cemetery Hill. Then Ferrero's USCT would follow them into battle and push on to capture Petersburg. Not surprisingly, the white troops were poorly prepared for this hastily assembled plan. Ledlie never instructed his brigade commanders that they were to capture the ridge at Cemetery Hill.[35]

After a delay (the fuses leading to the gunpowder fizzled out and had to be relit), the tremendous explosion finally occurred at 4:44 A.M. on July 30. The four tons of powder erupted, tearing an immense hole in the Confederate lines. The explosion launched earth, debris, men, and materiel hundreds of feet in the air, killing or wounding almost three hundred Rebels. Sergeant William H. Thomas of the Fifth USCT remembered the explosion as "a never to be forgotten sight of death and devastation."[36]

Ledlie's white division crawled slowly out of its trenches, followed by those of Willcox and Potter. But instead of dashing around the Crater and fanning out en route to high ground as Ferrero's division had been trained to do, the white troops stopped in the great Crater or became trapped in rifle pits to its right. The men quickly came under the intense fire of Confederates, who, because of the lethargy of Ledlie's men, had time to regroup. Amidst this chaos, Ferrero's four USCT regiments entered the fray. After unsuccessfully trying to skirt to the right, the black soldiers, led by the Forty-Third USCT, advanced beyond the Crater and engaged the Confederates in fierce hand-to-hand combat, capturing two hundred prisoners. Next came five USCT regiments of Colonel Henry Goddard Thomas's Second Brigade. These units, however, also soon became trapped in the Crater. "Our generals had pushed us into this slaughter pen," Lieutenant Robert Beecham of the Twenty-Third USCT remembered, "and then deserted us." Those soldiers not dead or dying crowded into the deadly pit.[37]

With their commanders preoccupied irresponsibly (Burnside and Meade exchanged hostile communications during the fight; Ledlie and Ferrero drank alcohol in a bombproof; Potter and Willcox stayed clear of the combat zone), the black troops, huddled and pinned down in the Crater, received withering enemy fire. By the time Burnside ordered a retreat, the Crater had become a hellish deathtrap for the exhausted, overheated, parched USCT. When Confederate infantrymen stormed the Crater, the blacks panicked and retreated, acting more like a stampeding mob than an army. According to one of its leaders, the USCT "became wild, confused, terror stricken, and . . . ran." Confederate riflemen picked off many of the black soldiers as they desperately tried to climb the steep sides of the hole. Some who tried to surrender were slaughtered; others were captured, never to reach the rear. It was a horrific sight. Lieutenant Colonel Delevan Bates of the Thirtieth USCT recalled that "Many a dusky warrior had his brains knocked out with the butt of a musket, or was run thru with a bayonet while vainly imploring for mercy." "Some of the Negro prisoners," Confederate General Edward Porter Alexander recollected, "who were originally allowed to surrender . . . were afterward shot by others, & there was, without doubt, a great deal of unnecessary killing of them."[38]

The Battle of the Crater, even more devastating than Fort Pillow, was the USCT's darkest hour, the war's "worst massacre." Forty-five hundred African Americans from Ferrero's Fourth Division entered the battle and 1,327 were hit. Four hundred and thirty-six black soldiers died. White soldiers suffered 2,471 casualties, including 227 deaths. The Twenty-Ninth USCT began the battle with 450 effectives and finished it with only 128. Writing two days after the disaster, General Grant described the battle as "the saddest affair I have witnessed in this war. Such opportunity for carrying fortifications I have never seen and do not expect again to have." In the aftermath of battle, soldiers and politicians alike pointed fingers, looking for scapegoats for the humiliating Union defeat. Not surprisingly, some blamed the black soldiers for the catastrophe.[39]

General Willcox, for example, praised the performance of his and Potter's divisions in the battle but reported that "Ledlie's division & the colored troops acted badly." A member of Willcox's staff agreed, remarking that the USCT "formed very well and advanced with much spirit till they came under hot fire, when they ignominiously broke and ran in every direction." Sergeant George F. Cram of the 105th Illinois Volunteer Infantry used their performance at the Crater as a justification to damn black men as soldiers. "What a pity! When so near the most brilliant victory ever known." Cram informed his mother that "the abolitionists may talk as they please, but I tell you that colored troops cannot be depended on and that evidently caused this great defeat."[40]

Burnside disagreed. Responding to questions posed by a court of inquiry, the general refused to hold the USCT responsible for the loss. Admitting "that the black troops broke and ran to the rear in considerable of a panic, which indicates misbehavior," Burnside nonetheless insisted that "they went in late, found in the enemy's works quite a mass of our own troops unable to advance, and during their formation, and in fact during their advance between the two lines, they were subjected to probably the hottest fire that any troops had been subjected to during the day." Burnside added that "I do not know that it is reasonable to suppose that after the loss of so great a portion of their officers they could have been expected to maintain their position." In his opinion, the black soldiers "certainly moved forward as gallantly under the first fire and until their ranks were broken as any troops I ever saw in action." After sifting the conflicting evidence, Congress's Joint Committee on the Conduct of the War blamed Meade for overruling Burnside's decision to use Ferrero's black troops to lead the attack. Ineptitude and mismanagement by Burnside, Grant, and Meade, however, not the USCT, caused the Union defeat at the Crater.[41]

The Crater disaster resulted in one benefit for the USCT, however. Following the debacle, General Benjamin F. Butler took steps to retaliate against Confederate abuse of blacks prisoners of war. When informed that the Rebels had placed 150 black prisoners to hard labor on Confederate fortifications under enemy fire, the general responded by placing the same number of Confederate prisoners under identical conditions. This did the trick. General Robert E. Lee ordered the blacks assigned to a prisoner-of-war camp and the Confederates never again employed blacks as slave laborers on the Richmond front.[42]

Though rumors of the USCT's poor showing at the Crater persisted, during the last months of the war no one accused the men of the USCT of cowardice. Frederick S. Eaton, an officer of the Thirty-Second USCT, informed readers of the *American Missionary*: "They can fight, have fought, are willing to fight, and in no instance have they proved unworthy the important position intrusted so judiciously to them." As the war drew to a close, the USCT repeatedly marched and fought hard in combat, demonstrating its value as soldiers and suffering severe losses.[43]

For example, on September 29, 1864, two brigades of General Charles J. Paine's Third Division, Eighteenth Corps, successfully assailed the Confederates' entrenched line of defense at New Market Heights, Virginia, north of the James River. This formidable position constituted a key element in the southeastern defenses of Richmond. Overcoming rough terrain, encountering many obstructions, and confronting galling fire, in two attacks the black troops captured the enemy's works and forced the Confederates to retreat. Following the engagement, one of the brigade commanders, Colonel Samuel A. Duncan, extolled the virtues of his men. "Ah! give me the Thunder-heads & Black hearts after all," Duncan wrote. "They fought splendidly . . . facing the red tempest of death with unflinching heroism." Another observer, the African American newspaper reporter

Thomas Morris Chester of the *Philadelphia Press*, complained that the USCT had received insufficient praise for its fighting at New Market Heights. "Every man looked like a soldier," Chester noted, "while inflexible determination was depicted upon every countenance. . . . Let us all be grateful that we have colored troops that will fight."[44]

No one came to appreciate the contributions of the USCT more so than President Lincoln, though he continued to justify their employment by military expediency and to pay scant attention to its meaning to the freedpeople. "So far as tested," the president announced in December 1863, "it is difficult to say they are not as good soldiers as any." In defensive language, no doubt intended for white supremacists who feared military emancipation, the president added: "No servile insurrection, or tendency to violence or cruelty, has marked the measures of emancipation and arming the blacks."[45] Five months later Lincoln remarked that the experiment of arming blacks "shows no loss by it in our foreign relations, none in our home popular sentiment, none in our white military force,—no loss by it any how or any where. On the contrary, it shows a gain of quite a hundred and thirty thousand soldiers, seamen, and laborers."[46]

Lincoln's critics of course saw things differently. Democrats, looking ahead to the November 1864 presidential election, charged that Lincoln's war for "nigger equality" had failed; the Crater had proved the futility of integrating the military. Not only Democrats, but conservative Republicans too, suggested that Lincoln rescind or limit the Emancipation Proclamation. The president was in a bind. He required conservative Republican support to win the election, but he needed the USCT to win the war.

During an August 1864 interview with former Wisconsin governor Alexander W. Randall and Judge Joseph T. Mills at the president's cottage at the Soldiers' Home, Lincoln remarked that some of his critics advocated that he return the slaves-turned-soldiers to their masters in order to conciliate the Confederates. "I should be damned in time & in eternity for so doing," Lincoln said. "The world shall know that I will keep my faith to friends & enemies, come what will. My enemies say I am now carrying on this war for the sole purpose of abolition. It is & will be carried on as long as I am President for the sole purpose of restoring the Union." Suppressing the rebellion and Lincoln's military emancipation project thus had become inseparable.[47]

"Any different policy in regard to the colored man," Lincoln explained a month later, deprives us of his help, and this is more than we can bear. We can not spare the hundred and forty or fifty thousand now serving us a soldiers, sailors, and laborers." Lincoln told Isaac M. Schermerhorn of Buffalo, New York, that his attitude toward black soldiers derived not from "sentiment or taste," but from military necessity, what the president termed "physical force which may be measured by and estimated as horse-power and Steam-power are measured and estimated. Keep it," he said, "and you can save the Union. Throw it away, and the Union goes with it." In no way would the blacks be "re-inslaved."[48]

Though in August Lincoln had predicted that "unless some great change takes place [I will be] *badly beaten*" in November, fortunately for him and the Union "great changes" did in fact occur. In September General William T. Sherman captured Atlanta, and a month later General Philip H. Sheridan successfully completed his Shenandoah Valley Campaign. These military victories swayed northern public opinion and helped Lincoln score a landslide victory over General George B. McClellan in November.[49] Lincoln showed his gratitude for the role the USCT was playing in suppressing the rebellion by selecting four companies of the Fifty-Fourth Massachusetts Volunteers as part of his military escort during his second inaugural. This was the first instance when black troops participated in an Inaugural Day parade.[50]

Following his reelection, two brigades of USCT proved themselves worthy of Lincoln's confidence by their heroic but deadly assaults on Confederate general John B. Hood's right flank at the Battle of Nashville, Tennessee (December 15–16, 1864). In his report of the battle, General James B. Steedman, after acknowledging that black troops suffered the highest casualties among his command, added: "I was unable to discover that color made any difference in the fighting of my troops. All, white and black, nobly did their duty as soldiers, and evinced cheerfulness and resolution such as I have never seen excelled in any campaign of the war in which I have borne a part."[51]

Though Steedman identified no difference between the military performance of white and black troops, the men of the USCT and their families still believed that the government treated them differently, less equitably, than white troops. As Jane Welcome, the mother of a Pennsylvanian in the Eighth USCT, explained in November 1864, "tha say that you will simpethise with the poor." Rosanna Henson, the wife of a soldier from New Jersey in the Twenty-Second USCT, complained to Lincoln that her husband, recuperating from a wound at the Macon House Hospital in Portsmouth, Virginia, had not been paid in over a year. "I write to you," Mrs. Henson noted, "because I have been told you would see to it. I have four children to support and I find this a great struggle. A hard life this! *I being a col^d woman do not get any State pay.* Yet my husband is fighting for the country."[52]

Following the July 1863 assault of the Fifty-Fourth Massachusetts Volunteers on Fort Wagner, the mother of a black soldier who fought in that battle corresponded with Lincoln. Writing from Buffalo, New York, Hannah Johnson told the president that before allowing her son to enlist, she had reflected on the possibility that he might be enslaved if captured by the Rebels, "but then they said M^r. Lincoln will never let them sell our colored solders for slaves, if they do he will get them back quck he will rettallyate and stop it." Responding to reports that Confederates were in fact reenslaving Union troops captured at Fort Wagner, Johnson asked, "Now Mr. Lincoln don't you think you oght to stop this thing and make them do the same by the colored men[?] they have lived in idleness all their lives on stolen labor and made savage[s] of the colored people, but they now are so furious because they are proving themselves to be men, such as have come away and got some education. It must not be so." She implored the president to "put the rebels to work in State prisons to making shoes and things, if they sell our colored soldiers, til they let them all go. And give their wounded the same treatment. it would seem cruel, but their no other way, and a just man must do hard things sometimes, that shew him to be a great man."[53]

Responding to rumors that Lincoln might "take back the [Emancipation] Proclamation," Johnson advised him, "don't do it." She explained, "When you are dead and in Heaven, in a thousand years that action of yours will make the Angels sing your praises I know it. Ought one man to own another, law for [lawful ?] or not who made the law, surely the poor slave did not. so it is wicked, and a horrible Outrage, there is no sense in it, because a man has lived by robbing all his life and his father before him, should he complain because the stolen things found on him are taken[?]" Johnson informed Lincoln that "Robbing the colored people of their labor is but a small part of the robbery their souls are almost taken, they are made bruits of often. You know all about this." Finally she urged the president to ensure "that the colored men fighting now, are fairly treated. You ought to do this, and do it at once, Not let the thing run along meet it quickly and manfully, and stop this, mean cowardly cruelty. We poor oppressed ones, appeal to you, and ask fair play."[54]

* * *

Such heartrending requests raise the question as to the degree to which Lincoln directly interacted with the men of the USCT. He first formally observed black soldiers in April 1864, when in a dress parade of General Ambrose E. Burnside's Ninth Army Corps, as it marched through Washington, D.C., en route from Annapolis, Maryland, to join the Army of the Potomac at Brandy Station, on the Virginia front. The Ninth consisted of more than six regiments of USCT recruited in Connecticut, Maryland, Ohio, and Pennsylvania. The occasion allowed the black troops to pay "their respects" to Lincoln as they marched in new uniforms, reportedly "looking as smart and martial as any." The soldiers paraded down New York Avenue and halted at Fourteenth Street, turning south to pass Willard's Hotel, a few blocks from the White House. Lieutenant Colonel H. Seymour Hall of the Forty-Third USCT recalled proudly that his men, only recently trained in battalion drill and in the manual of arms, marched like veterans. He remembered that "the crowd of spectators gave us loud and prolonged applause."[55]

Charles Coffin of the *Boston Journal* also observed the president's review of the Ninth. He reported that Lincoln, standing on a balcony with Burnside, acknowledged the black soldiers with "dignified kindness and courtesy." But the raw recruits became ecstatic upon spotting the president, the emancipator of their race, towering above them on Willard's balcony. "They swing their caps, clap their hands and shout their joy," Coffin recalled. "Long, loud and jubilant are the rejoicings of these redeemed sons of Africa." According to another observer, the black soldiers saluted "gracefully with their colors and [gave] loud hurrahs for the Great Emancipator of their race."[56]

Two months later General Grant invited the commander in chief to his headquarters to review General Edward W. Hinks's USCT division, Army of the James, at City Point, Virginia. These troops had fought with distinction in General William F. Smith's assault on Confederate forts at Petersburg on June 15. Lincoln left Washington in the evening of June 20 aboard the steamer the *City of Baltimore*, arriving at Deep Bottom the next morning eager for the chance to visit the black soldiers. The president informed Grant that his intent was to "take a look at the brave fellows who have fought their way down to Petersburg in this wonderful campaign." Grant loaned Lincoln his reddish brown thoroughbred, "Cincinnati," and the men, accompanied by Grant's staff, headed toward the troops. General Horace Porter, Grant's aide, remarked that the president, though an accomplished horsemen, "was not a very dashing rider" and appeared "grotesque," riding awkwardly amid the soldiers. Lincoln was conspicuous on horseback in his proverbial tall black silk hat, frock coat, and trousers that rode up his long legs, making him resemble "a country farmer riding into town wearing his Sunday clothes." Another observer wrote that Lincoln had the appearance "of a professional undertaker cracking a dry joke." By the time he reached the troops, Lincoln's black attire was so dusty that his outfit appeared to be no longer black, but Confederate gray.[57]

According to General Porter, the black troops responded to Lincoln's presence with unrestrained emotion. "The enthusiasm of the blacks now knew no limits," Porter wrote, "They cheered, laughed, cried, sang hymns of praise and shouted in their negro dialect, 'God bress Massa Linkum!' 'De Lord save Fader Abraham!' 'De day ob jubilee am come shuuah.'" The men of the USCT, enthusiastic to see the president, lined the road, broke ranks, and crowded around him. They reportedly cheered, cried, kissed his hands, laughed, and touched Lincoln's clothes. Rendered speechless by the men's adulation, Lincoln bowed and lifted his hat in a salute with tears in his eyes. According to Sylvanus Cadwallader, the Wisconsin-born war correspondent for the *Chicago Times*, the blacks' response "was a genuine spontaneous outburst of love and affection for the man they looked upon as their deliverer from bondage." His encounters with the men of the USCT brought Lincoln "face-to-face with the reality of the revolution he had helped to make."[58]

In another instance, in March 1865, Lincoln reviewed the First Division of the all-black Twenty-Fifth Corps, Army of the James, then commanded by General Godfery Weitzel, near Petersburg. Again deeply moved by and impressed with the sight of the well-drilled men of the USCT, the president reportedly quipped, "I wonder how Jeff [Davis] would like to have such colored troops in his army!"[59]

Quartermaster Sergeant John C. Brock of the Forty-Third USCT recalled how he had stood proudly at attention when Lincoln reviewed his men at City Point on the James River. The soldiers waited from late morning to mid-afternoon for the president's appearance, again astride Grant's horse. An aide later reported that the "manifestation of strength on the part of the splendid Army of the James" boosted Lincoln's spirits. Brock remarked how the men of the USCT viewed Lincoln "with the holy awe and reverence which was due him who was the nation's pride, as well as the bondsman's savior." "How little did we think that in one short month he would be no more." Brock did see Lincoln one more time, however.[60]

George Washington Williams, the USCT veteran who wrote the first documented history of black military service in the war, considered Lincoln's review of the black soldiers at City Point "one of the most magnificent military spectacles of the civil war." He described it in detail: "The weather was fair and the atmosphere pleasant for the moving masses of troops. Twenty-five thousand Negro soldiers, in bright, new uniforms, well drilled, well armed, and well officered, passed in review before the President, General Grant, and the general officers of the Army of the James and the Army of the Potomac. . . . The troops marched with company front, with banners flying and bands flying. Nearly every slave State had its representatives in the ranks of this veteran Negro army." Williams reported that Lincoln "was deeply moved at the sight of these Negro troops, against whose employment he had early and earnestly protested." Other observers, including hundreds of white officers and their men, praised what Williams termed "the soldierly bearing of their Negro comrades in arms."[61]

On another occasion, Secretary of State William H. Seward and one of Lincoln's secretaries, William O. Stoddard, were walking in Washington and observed a unit of black recruits parading. Stoddard recalled in 1866, "They were really a fine looking body of men, and marched well for such new recruits." When asked his opinion of the USCT, Seward replied, "It grows, it grows." President Lincoln, who also had observed the column of black soldiers from a White House window, responded to the same query, "It'll do, it'll do!"[62] When observing parading columns of the USCT, Lincoln conveyed an important political message, both to the troops and to the nation at large. He treated black soldiers with consummate respect, just as he respected white troops. The men of the USCT deserved respect. They were men and they fought, sacrificed, and died for their country.[63]

As the war dragged on, Lincoln recognized that African Americans had become an invaluable resource to the Union military effort and had earned the rights and privileges of other Americans. The commander in chief admitted that though he had not set out to free and arm the slaves, circumstances warranted his actions. "I claim not to have controlled events," he explained to Kentucky editor Albert G. Hodges in 1864, "but confess plainly that events have controlled me." Uncertain of the future, Lincoln looked for divine guidance. "If God now wills the removal of a great wrong, and wills also that we . . . shall pay fairly for our complicity in that wrong, impartial history will find therein new cause to attest and revere the justice and goodness of God."[64]

Lincoln's prayers, as well as those of the nation, finally were answered when, in April 1865, Richmond fell to Union troops. Soon after, General Lee surrendered his army to Grant. Ten regiments of the USCT were among the first federal units to liberate the Rebel seat of government on the morning of April 3. Richmond's population of ten thousand blacks found the presence of black troops in their midst almost overpowering. A soldier in Company B, Ninth USCT, recorded the scene: "Drums beating, colors flying and men singing the John Brown hymn—Gloria in excelsis!"[65]

Lincoln arrived in Richmond a day later to survey the fallen Confederate capital. "Later still do we remember," Quartermaster Sergeant Brock recalled, "on the second day after our triumphant entry into the boasted stronghold of Rebeldom, the booming cannon announced the arrival of our illustrious President, whose heart was then overjoyed to think that his trials and troubles concerning this wicked rebellion would soon be ended." Lincoln's Richmond visit signified for black persons what one historian terms "the fulfillment of biblical messianic prophecy; seeing him in person confirmed their freedom." Like Brock, the Reverend Garland H. White, chaplain of the Twenty-Eighth USCT and himself a former slave, also observed Lincoln in Richmond during its first days of Federal occupation. "I never saw so many colored people in all my life, women and children of all sizes running after Father, or Master Abraham, as they called him."[66]

Reporter Thomas Morris Chester similarly explained in the *Philadelphia Press* that when Richmond's blacks spotted Lincoln, "their joy knew no bounds." As Lincoln toured the war-torn former Confederate capital crowds of blacks surrounded him. "The colored population was wild with enthusiasm. Old men thanked God in a very boisterous manner, and old women shouted upon the pavement as high as they had ever done at a religious revival." Chester noted that some slaves, confined prior to sale in Richmond's notorious slave pens, were incredulous about their new freedom until they saw the Union troops and President Lincoln. A female slave declared: "I know that I am free, for I have seen Father Abraham and felt him."[67]

AFTERWORD

At two o'clock on Wednesday, April 19, 1865, five days following President Abraham Lincoln's assassination, Washington's church bells tolled. A hearse drawn by six gray horses carried the dead president's body in the two-hour-long funeral procession down Pennsylvania Avenue from the White House to the Capitol, where the open coffin was to lie in state in the Rotunda. Three hundred men of the Twenty-Second USCT, a battle-tested regiment recruited in Philadelphia, traveled overnight to Washington, fresh from the Virginia front. Once arriving in the capital city, the black unit accidentally positioned itself at the front of the long funeral cortege.

With the street filled with marchers and the sidewalks overrun with onlookers, the Twenty-Second could not reposition itself. Unable to redirect the black troops, the parade marshals, "swallowing hard, decided to let them lead the way." The USCT unit, considered by its commander General Godfrey Weitzel to be one of his best, halted, wheeled into column, reversed its arms and stood at "rest." According to an observer, "the band struck up a dirge, and the regiment immediately moved forward, thereby becoming the head of the procession." A newspaperman reported that the black soldiers "appeared to be under the very best discipline, and displayed admirable skill in their various exercises." A mile to the rear, thousands of African Americans trailed along in their accustomed place, in the back.[1] The *New York Times* reported that "their walk and their mien were the very impersonation of sorrow." Three days later, the

Twenty-Second USCT boarded a boat at Charles County, Maryland, to join in the hunt for Lincoln's assassin.[2]

The irony and symbolic meaning of black soldiers leading the procession, and then participating in the search for Lincoln's murderer, would not have been lost on the deceased chief executive. By the end of the war, the president had developed a special interest in the accomplishments of the men of the USCT, a force that his supporters increasingly identified as one of the landmark achievements of his first administration and that his critics considered an insult to whites and a harbinger of racial equality and miscegenation. As the war unfolded, Lincoln "had staked the credibility of his racial policies on their performance."[3]

To be sure, Lincoln had freed the Confederacy's slaves with his pen, but they had helped to suppress the rebellion with their military service. Lincoln relied on free African Americans to draw the slaves to Union lines and to add almost 180,000 men to the Federal forces. Though the president had limited direct contact with people of color, following his death they came to consider him their emancipator, father, friend, and leader. For example, the indefatigable and redoubtable Harriet Tubman, Civil War nurse, recruiter, scout, and spy, had criticized Lincoln's appeasement of slaveholders early in the war; his lethargy in freeing and arming the slaves; and later his foot-dragging in equalizing the USCT's pay. Three decades later, however, Tubman appreciated fully what Lincoln had done for her people. "Yes, I'se sorry now I didn't see Massa Lincoln and tank him," she said.[4]

Many African Americans transformed Lincoln into their Messiah, a Christ-like figure, as God's instrument for freeing the slaves.[5] For instance, in May 1865 Orderly Sergeant James C. Taylor of the Ninety-Third USCT pronounced that "God, in his divine wisdom, through the instrumentality of our noble President, Abraham Lincoln, saw fit to remove, the only dark spot (Slavery) from one of the most glorious flags the sun ever shone upon." Six months later I. N. Triplett, formerly an orderly sergeant in the Sixtieth USCT, proposed a resolution on the late president at a convention of black veterans in Iowa. Triplett mourned "the sad fate of the martyr President, Abraham Lincoln, the great Emancipator, and devoted friend of our race, yet rejoice that the great work which God appointed him to perform has been so nearly accomplished that the wrath of the oppressor is utterly powerless to prevent a full and glorious consummation."[6]

To a certain extent Lincoln had considered himself the vehicle for freeing the slaves, arming blacks, and helping them to assert themselves as men. In April 1865 he modestly told Lieutenant Daniel H. Chamberlain of the all-black Fifth Massachusetts Cavalry, and later Reconstruction governor of South Carolina, "I have only been an instrument" of ending slavery. "The logic and moral power of [William Lloyd] Garrison and the anti-slavery people of the country and the army have done all." Like Moses, Lincoln was a deliverer.[7]

Though black soldiers and their families found frustrating and insulting the hardships and inequalities they had endured, during the war and for many decades following emancipation, African Americans generally revered Lincoln as their great emancipator. In their 1863 report to the secretary of war, the commissioners of the American Freedmen's Inquiry Commission stated, "Our Chief Magistrate would probably be surprised to learn with what reverence, bordering on superstition, he is regarded by these poor people." The commissioners described a conversation among a group of black stevedores in Beaufort, South Carolina, who lauded Lincoln's seemingly majestic power over their former masters and were predicting what he would do for their race. Suddenly an elderly black man, "a 'praise man' (as the phrase is) amongst them, with all the solemnity and earnestness of an old prophet, broke forth: What do you know 'bout Massa Linkum? Massa Linkum be ebrewhere. He walk de earth like de Lord."[8] Recruiting men for the USCT in Huntsville, Alabama, in 1864, a heavy-handed conscription agent tried to convince a black recruit's wife why he should join up. "Father Abraham don't want women and haint sent me after them. . . . I want your man." The mere mention of Lincoln's name, at least according to the recruiter, evoked respect and obedience.[9]

In 1864 one of Lincoln's commanders in Arkansas put the men of the Fifty-Seventh USCT to work constructing fortifications and earthworks. He wrote the president, "I told them the other day I thought if they made a good fort of it we would call it Fort Lincoln which greatly pleased the men and made them shovel faster." In 1866 veterans of two Missouri USCT regiments, the Sixty-Second and Sixty-Fifth, considered advancing black education the best way to honor Lincoln. They raised $5,000 toward the founding of Lincoln Institute (today Lincoln University) in Jefferson City. In 1890 William Murrell, born a slave in Georgia in 1845 and a veteran of the 138th USCT, proclaimed at a New Jersey encampment of the Grand Army of the Republic that "the name of Lincoln, with the Negroes of America, will never die; we love his name; we love his memory." Lincoln, Murrell added, "struck the shackles from four millions of human beings. I was one from whom the shackles fell."[10]

Decades later, Angie Garrett, who had been a slave in Alabama, recalled that though "I never seed Mr. Lincoln, but when they told me 'bout him, I thought he was partly God." Another former slave, Aunt Pinkey Howard of El Dorado, Arkansas, described Lincoln and the black soldiers who liberated her people: "Oooh, child," Howard told an interviewer, "you ought to been here when Mr. Linktum come down to free us. Policemen ain't in it. You ought to seen them big black bucks. Their suits was so fine trimmed with them eagle buttons and they was gold too. And their shoes shined so they hurt your eyes."[11] An analysis of 1,846 interviews of former slaves during the 1930s concluded that of 306 former bondsmen who commented on Lincoln, 18 percent (fifty-five comments) identified the president with emancipation while 14 percent (forty-three comments) interpreted Lincoln as God's instrument. These associations were the two most often expressed by former slaves about Lincoln.[12] Today, Africans American continue to attribute Lincoln's greatness to emancipation. And public representations of the USCT remain among the few consistently positive interpretations linking Lincoln to African Americans in the American imagination.[13]

The president's assassination hit most Americans, even white southerners, like a flash of lightning, but it hit no others as hard as it did African Americans, especially men who had served in the USCT. "His death burdened every black with a personal sense of loss," wrote historian Benjamin Quarles. The black troops credited the president with freeing their brethren—he was their "Great Emancipator"—and as the man who gave them their chance to be free and to fight the Rebels. Lincoln occupied a special place "in the hearts and minds of Afro-Americans," writes an authority on the USCT. The black troops considered Lincoln's assassination "a bit more personal than that of most other Federal troops." Their white officers also judged Lincoln's death an especially severe blow.[14]

For example, a junior officer in the USCT explained to his wife, "I am getting to regard Old Abe almost as a *Father*—to almost venerate him—so earnestly do I believe in his earnestness, fidelity, honesty & Patriotism. I begin to look upon him some as the ancient Jews did upon Moses—as a chosen instrument of God for the deliverance of the Nation." Lieutenant George L. Gaskill of the Eleventh U.S. Colored Heavy Artillery explained to his sister: "I cannot paint to you the grief and indignation that our officers feel. With us of the U.S. Colored Army the death of Lincoln is indeed the loss of a friend. From him we received our commission—and toward him we have even looked as toward a Father." Major James Madison Bowler of the 113th USCT, posted in Little Rock, Arkansas, pledged to fight the conspirators who murdered Lincoln "with good will till I die, if necessary." He instructed his wife, Lizzie, in Minnesota to "Kiss Baby for me. Learn her to speak and revere the name of Abraham Lincoln, the people's friend."[15]

An officer of the Forty-First USCT, then stationed south of Petersburg, recalled how the sad news of Lincoln's murder "cast a gloom over our camp," adding "and one could see and hear the grief of those poor colored men over his tragic end." Just days before, the regiment had been in Richmond during the president's visit to the former Confederate capital. According to an enlisted man in the Eleventh U.S. Colored Heavy Artillery, word of Lincoln's assassination "fell upon our company like a thunderbolt. Many hope that it was just another false rumor." "Nothing has so shocked us so much as the death of this patriot and statesman," explained Sergeant Charles H. Davis of the 108th USCT. Davis extolled the assassinated president as "oppressed Americans' friend." African Americans would long continue to "cherish his name as a household word. His image will be fixed in the hearts of four millions for whom he spoke the word of freedom, and who will mourn for him with great grief."[16] Dr. Anderson Ruffin

Abbott, a Canadian-born free black man who came to know Lincoln during his service as acting assistant surgeon at Washington's Freedmen's Hospital, paid his respects to the fallen president as he lay in state at the White House. Abbott looked into the dead leader's face, and "a great sorrow weighed heavily upon his heart, for he thought of the loss to the negro race in their nascent life of freedom, and the great guiding hand that now lay paralyzed in death."[17]

When writing about their late lamented commander in chief, black soldiers commonly invoked religious symbols. "As Soldiers in the US Service we mourn the loss of our Noble Chief Magistrate. We have looked to him as our earthly Pilot to guide us through this National Storm and Plant us Securely on the Platform of Liberty, and Equal Political right," extolled the Reverend Chauncey B. Leonard, reportedly the first black chaplain to be commissioned by Lincoln during the war.[18] "Humanity has lost a firm advocate, our race its Patron Saint, and the good of all the world a fitting object to emulate," wrote Edward Dinsmore of the Fifty-Fifth Massachusetts Volunteers, stationed in Charleston in May 1865. "Shurely while we mourn this great calamity we have some slight consolation in the belief that he is rewarded for his labours here, in that land where sin cometh not, and sorrow is unknown. The name of Abraham Lincoln will ever be cherished in our hearts, and none will more delight to lisp his name in reverence than the future generations of our people."[19]

"Lincoln was indeed our Moses," recalled a USCT veteran. "He gave us our freedom." Others echoed the words of a freedman on South Carolina's Hilton Head Island who proclaimed: "Lincoln died for we, Christ died for we, and me believe him de same mans." When a young black boy informed his elders that he wanted to see the president, an elderly man replied: "'No man see Linkum. Linkum walk as Jesus walk. No man see Linkum.'" A group of black soldiers struggled to find a way to thank Lincoln. "We cannot express in words our love for the President of the United States, as language is too weak to convey that estimation in which we hold him," they said. When, during the 1864 siege of Petersburg, a brigade of USCT spotted Lincoln and his entourage, the black soldiers broke ranks and greeted him with shouts of "Hurrah for the Liberator, Hurrah for the President."[20]

Elijah P. Marrs, born a slave in Shelby County, Kentucky, in 1840, learned to read and write while working on a farm with about thirty other bondsmen and bondswomen. Committed to join the northern army to fight for "principle and freedom," Marrs enlisted in the Twelfth U.S. Colored Artillery in September 1864, and, because of his literacy, he was appointed duty sergeant. Marrs learned of the president's assassination while leading a patrol outside Bowling Green, Kentucky. He recalled: "I marched my men out on the plain and sat down and wept. We remained there until nightfall, and then returned to the town and joined with the men in camp in sorrowing over our loss. Our Moses had been slain, and we knew not what the future had in store for us."[21]

Perhaps it was only fitting that on April 20, 1865, just five days following Lincoln's death, Major Martin R. Delany, 104th USCT, proposed the erection of a national monument to honor the martyred president. Delany was a remarkable man. The Harvard-educated physician, African explorer, novelist, editor, abolitionist, and Pan-Africanist, had served as a recruiting agent for the USCT in the North; he attained national prominence by meeting alone with Lincoln on February 8, 1865. Delany and the president shared a long interest in and a commitment to resettling the South's slaves to Africa.

According to Delany's nineteenth-century biographer Frank A. Rollin, during that interview, Delany captivated Lincoln by proposing that the government mobilize an independent all-black army composed of the USCT, supplemented by freed slaves, and officered by black men. Delany modeled his proposed "corps d'Afrique" on a Berber tribe in Algeria. It would live off the land and utilize guerrilla tactics to subdue the Rebels and free their slaves. Lincoln reportedly was so taken with Delany's plan that he immediately recommended that Secretary of War Edwin M. Stanton commission him as a line officer in the infantry, assigning him to recruit black troops under the command of General Rufus B. Saxton in South Carolina.[22] Regardless of the accuracy of Rollin's account (a recent student labels it "extravagant in its claims but revealing in its strategy"), Delany did in fact receive a commission as major in the U.S. Infantry and went on to recruit black troops under Saxton.[23] Delany was one of fewer than one hundred black men to receive an officer's commission in the Union army, holding the highest rank among them. He later served as sub-assistant commissioner of the Freedmen's Bureau in South Carolina.

Summarizing a speech Major Delany delivered before a black audience soon after receiving his commission, a white journalist remarked: "The speaker claimed that he was authorized to set the Government right before the people! He told his brethren that they had no reason to complain—that the Government intended to deal justly and fairly with them—that it would commission colored officers when they were qualified—that it would treat colored soldiers well—and finally that it intended to make no distinctions between white and black soldiers." The reporter added: "The speaker scouted the idea of social equality."[24]

In his proposal to honor Lincoln, Delany appealed for blacks to fund a monument to the martyred president as a token of their respect and gratitude, lauding Lincoln as "the humane, the benevolent, the philanthropic, the generous, the beloved, the able, the wise, great, and good man, the President of the United States, ABRAHAM LINCOLN, the Just." He suggested that if all persons of color, north and south, contributed one cent each toward the monument, they could raise $40,000 toward enshrining Lincoln at an appropriate site in Illinois. The proposed monument, according to Delany, would serve as "a just and appropriate tribute of respect and lasting gratitude from the colored people of the United States to the memory of President Lincoln, the Father of American Liberty." In June 1865, Delany published a second article on his proposed Lincoln monument, including details for its design and erection. Decorative tear drops would signify the four million African Americans who wept "for the great and good deliverer of their race from bondage in the United States." The Reverend Elisha Weaver, the influential editor of the *Christian Recorder*, the organ of the African Methodist Episcopal Church, endorsed Delany's proposed monument to Lincoln. His fellow black Americans should pay tribute to the late president, he wrote, honoring "the name of one who sacrificed every thing, even life itself, in defending the rights of down-trodden humanity."[25]

Three weeks following Lincoln's assassination, Quartermaster Sergeant John C. Brock of the Forty-Third U.S. Colored Infantry published a deeply felt eulogy of the martyred president. Born in

1843, Brock was a native of Carlisle, Pennsylvania, and enlisted in the USCT in April 1864. His regiment served in the Army of the Potomac in the 1864 Wilderness Campaign, fought at the Battle of the Crater, performed fatigue labor at Petersburg, and then participated in engagements at Poplar Grove Church, Hatcher's Run, and Bermuda Hundred, before being assigned to the First Division, Twenty-Fifth Corps. Religious, literate, and articulate, Brock exhibited leadership skills and was promoted first to commissary sergeant and then to quartermaster sergeant. As a series of articles that he published in the *Christian Recorder* suggests, Brock devoted himself first to overthrowing slavery and then to obtaining full and equal rights for people of color. He took special pride in the fact that black troops had played leading roles in liberating the slaves.[26]

Speaking for the men of the USCT and for all black Americans, Sergeant Brock praised Lincoln as a "fearless patriot," a "wise statesman," a "skilful pilot, who . . . guided the ship of state safely through the storm of four long years of unparalleled war, turmoil and bloodshed." Lincoln's name was a watchword for all Americans, according to Brock, but no more so than for "the lowly slave in the far distant south, who would speak of him with reverence and wait with longing eyes, for the representatives of him, to whom they looked as the guardian angel to release them from the thraldoms of bondage." Brock eulogized the president's patience, his determination and willingness to hold fast against treason, while others doubted him, to the principles of Union and freedom. He thanked God that Lincoln lived long enough to witness "with his eagle eye rebellion crushed, the supremacy of the government re-established, Slavery forever blotted from off the statute books of America."[27]

Like many African Americans, Brock maintained that the president had given up his life for their freedom. "Although he is taken away from us, his acts of kindness and deeds of philanthropy will live through all eternity." Brock urged the men of the USCT, as well as their wives and families, not to mourn their lost leader. "Your Chieftain is not dead, he still lives," Brock explained. "He lives in the thousands of brave soldiers, who still keep step to the music of the Union, who are resolved to see that flag, he loved so well, planted victoriously over every foot of American soil, who are bound to see his great principle of Union and Liberty carried out to the letter, who are bound to see that treason is trampled out from off the face of this Union, never more to rise; who will take care to see that all rebellious, cowardly assassins receive their due reward." Brock believed that Lincoln's spirit would live on "in the hearts of those bereaved wives and children, whose husbands, fathers and brothers have been struck down by the fell hand of the rebellion, whose universal cry is that this rebellion must be subdued, and traitors receive their due reward."[28] After serving with the Forty-Third USCT at Brownsville, Texas, Brock mustered out of service in October 1865.

While numerous men of the USCT, both during their service and later as veterans, praised Lincoln for emancipating and arming members of their race, some judged the president as too conservative, too accommodating to the forces of white supremacy and the racial status quo. For example, during the 1864 presidential election, "Africano," probably a trooper in the Fifth Massachusetts Colored Cavalry, though clearly preferring Lincoln over Democratic candidate George B. McClellan, nonetheless faulted the president for stopping short of ending slavery unequivocally when he had the chance to do so in January 1863. "Africano" listed the reasons he refused to be identified as a "Lincolnite."

> 1st, Mr. Lincoln's unjust policy towards the negro soldiers in not enforcing upon the rebel authorities the necessity of acknowledging and treating them as prisoners of war.
> 2d, His partial freedom and his colonization scheme.
> 3d, His ordering the enlistment of slaves and paying the bounty to their so-called masters, under pretense of being loyal men, thereby recognizing, to a certain extent, the right of property in man.
> 4th, His protecting disloyal Kentucky and parts of greater disloyal States from the liberating influence of his double-sided instrument.

Though "Africano" had serious reservations about Lincoln, he quipped, "for the time being we shall carefully avoid intermingling him with baser coin." While many African American soldiers had expressed doubts about Lincoln, he nevertheless was their clear choice over McClellan in 1864.[29] In 1901 William H. Thomas, formerly a sergeant in the Fifth USCT, recalled fondly casting his first vote, for Lincoln, in 1864.[30]

To be sure, Lincoln had appeared to be contradictory, tentative, and vacillating in shaping his emancipation project. The president's seeming lethargy is unsurprising when one considers that the freeing and then arming of the slaves brought into conflict two basic tenets of American life—democratic ideals and white racism. The Civil War signified a revolutionary moment in American history, and recasting Lincoln's emancipation dilemma in late-twentieth-century civil rights ideology constitutes dangerous presentism.

Always opposed to slavery on economic and humanitarian grounds, Lincoln as president confronted complex constitutional questions of sovereignty and law. Hence, when the Civil War began, circumstances forced Lincoln to tread lightly and move slowly in treating the "peculiar institution." From the war's start to the summer of 1862, the president proceeded cautiously and pragmatically, some said haltingly, determined to find a way to keep the Union intact, while respecting slaveholders' property, keeping the border states, notably Kentucky, in the Union, and defeating armed insurgents in the South. This was a tall order. Over time he not only emancipated but armed the slaves of Rebels and opened service in the military to free blacks throughout the nation.

During the course of a year and a half, Lincoln moved from rejecting the freeing of the slaves as war measure, to transforming Union troops into the liberators of the South's 4 million enslaved men, women, and children. Early in the war Lincoln instructed his field commanders to return fugitive slaves first to Rebel masters, then to return them only to loyal slaveholders, and then finally to return none, designating fugitive slaves "contraband of war"—and employing them as laborers. Thanks to the Militia Act and the Second Confiscation Act of July 1862, even before the final Emancipation Proclamation, however, Congress had authorized the president to utilize slaves militarily as he saw fit. He hesitated, mobilizing only several thousand black soldiers in a catch-as-catch-can way. Only after January 1863 did Lincoln call former slaves and free blacks to arms, spurring them to defeat the slaveholding insurrectionists. In doing so, they, more so than Lincoln per se, radically altered American race relations and the course of American history.

To Lincoln's credit, once the president settled squarely on freeing and then arming the blacks, he moved ahead without reservation. Slavery ended thanks to Lincoln and to the almost 180,000 black soldiers that he mobilized to snuff it out. "From defining the war's purpose as the reestablishment of a Union committed to no more than a gradual melting away of the peculiar institution, he had moved to champion a nation energized by the prospect of slavery's imminent and permanent removal."[31]

In August 1864, Lincoln defended himself against a Democratic editor who charged that his emancipation policies contradicted the language of his public letter to Horace Greeley two years earlier. The president, underscoring the seriousness of the matter, and dismissing rhetoric, argued that the Union would not have been preserved "by magic, or miracles, but by inducing the colored people to come bodily over from the rebel side to ours." He went on to justify freeing and arming the blacks in the most pragmatic of terms. "It is not a question of sentiment or taste, but one of physical force, which may be measured, and estimated." The military support of African Americans, Lincoln reasoned, "is more than we can lose, and live."[32]

Unquestionably, the president valued the service of the men of the USCT greatly. Their military contribution proved Lincoln's confidence in them to be well deserved and disarmed whites' fears of black insurrection and mayhem. While Lincoln's final Emancipation Proclamation liberated and armed the slaves on paper, it was the men of the USCT who welcomed them to their camps and liberated (sometimes by force) slaves on farms and plantations as they enveloped the Confederacy. They, not Lincoln, "fought directly for the freedom that Lincoln had promised."[33]

On balance, Lincoln's military emancipation program was a great success, one of the transformative events in American history. No plan by a chief executive had more immediate and long-lasting impact on American history and character. Though spirited less by ideology and a sense of racial justice than by pragmatism and military necessity, the president's twin policies of freeing and arming America's slaves nevertheless accomplished multiple goals. It also signaled Lincoln's emerging understanding of the expanded powers of the executive branch of government.

Indeed, Lincoln's decision to mobilize black troops was a wise strategic move. Military emancipation helped fill Union armies, so much so that Richard Slotkin considers it "difficult to see how the war could have been won without their addition to the armed forces." The president's emancipation initiative also jolted the South's agricultural economy by inspiring Confederate slaves to escape and opening new doors to freedom and the prospect of equality. The recruiting of black men in the South's plantation districts sounded an alarm for slaves to set flight for freedom and the Union blue. The mere presence of the USCT in areas where slaves still labored for Confederate or loyal masters disrupted the institution's operation. Black enlistment caused economic chaos among southern whites, resulting in labor shortages, loss of capitalized labor, and reduced crop production. Lincoln's emancipation edict gave slaves a clear message that northern victory would translate into their freedom. Recent scholars, like W. E. B. Du Bois decades ago, interpret the Emancipation Proclamation as fomenting "a slow-motion slave insurrection on the largest scale—masses of slaves leaving their home plantations to seek freedom within Union army lines. By detaching slaves from masters the Proclamation undermined and eventually destroyed the South's system of production."[34]

Unquestionably, military recruitment disrupted slavery and farm and plantation operations, creating a dearth of laborers for which masters generally were not compensated. It dampened the spirits of the Rebels to fight on near the end of the war; signaled the death knell of slavery, especially in the border states where the Emancipation Proclamation had been excluded; and provided a platform for agency, citizenship, and self-assertion by the freed people. For the first time in American history, African Americans could serve in the national army, long considered to be a citizen's right and responsibility.

Mobilizing the USCT began the process of extending civil rights to thousands of black males. In combat, black men "proved that they could make good soldiers—and thus good citizens."[35]

Beyond these implications, Lincoln's emancipation project gave African Americans pragmatic reasons for fighting, literally, to preserve the Union. During the first two years of the war, northern black communities had little interest in and impact on war policy. That changed after 1863. Lincoln's military enlistment program boosted civilian morale, especially that of northern free blacks. Black communities took immense pride in their homegrown troops. Women's auxiliaries sewed their flags and undergarments and held picnics and socials to raise money for their troops, sending them food and supplies and sharing with them love and support. By inviting them to fight, Lincoln granted blacks part ownership in the war and, accordingly, he had to pay attention to "their interests and even their opinions." In being now free and armed, black men in turn became part of the president's "Unionist coalition." In short, military emancipation signified "a major milestone in the relationship between the federal government and black men, both free and soon to be freed."[36]

Service in the USCT also broadened, educated, and provided slaves and free blacks entrée to bigger worlds. Bethuel Hunter writes, "The war introduced these men to worlds of experience far beyond the marginalized existence many had known as freemen and the repression others had suffered under slavery. Where opportunity, however circumscribed, presented itself, those with initiative acquired rudimentary education and developed skills in leadership. But the price they paid collectively can never be tabulated. The war shattered the bodies and psyches of some of these men. And it steeled the determination of others for the sterner tests that lay ahead."[37] Three months after Appomattox, Sergeant Henry J. Maxwell, Second U.S. Colored Light Artillery, addressed the Convention of the Colored Men of Tennessee in Nashville. "We want the rights guaranteed by the Infinite Architect," Maxwell declared. "For these rights we labor; for them we will die. We have gained one—the uniform is its badge. We want two more boxes, beside the cartridge box—the ballot box and the jury box."[38]

Despite its major importance in shattering the bonds of slavery and democratizing America, one must be careful not to romanticize Lincoln's military emancipation project. Many contemporary African Americans and their white friends, eager to prove blacks' worthiness for postwar civil and political rights, exaggerated the role of the USCT in attaining Union victory. In 1887, for example, the popular black journalist John Edward Bruce lavished praise on the "colored soldier" who, "by his coolness, steadiness, and determined courage and dash . . . silenced every cavil of doubt of their soldierly capacity and drawn tokens of great admiration from their enemies." A veteran of the Twenty-Fifth U.S. Cavalry agreed, stating, "There were no braver men that shouldered a musket than the colored soldier." And in 1906, Burt G. Wilder, a distinguished white physician who served on the medical staff of the Fifty-Fifth Massachusetts Volunteers, celebrated the USCT's "valor and initiative."[39] More recently, two writers lauded the saga of the USCT as one of "Race, Patriotism, and Glory," in which the African Americans displayed "unmatched bravery and uncommon valor."[40]

While it is easy to overstate the USCT's across-the-board military performance, even to render it heroic, historian William A. Dobak contextualizes it. "The project of putting black men in uniform inspired modest hopes, at best, in most white Americans. Any evidence of black soldiers' courage and resolve led to wild enthusiasm among their supporters and often to gross exaggeration." Despite many doubters, they eventually earned the nation and Lincoln's trust, first as garrison troops in the Departments of the South and the Gulf and in the Mississippi drainage basin, and later when engaged in heavy combat in Virginia and North Carolina. They performed well especially in geographical areas they knew best and when well trained and officered. Dobak remarks that the USCT met with less success when thrown into assaults on enemy trenches. The men "clearly had little trouble carrying out assignments when they relied on knowledge they already possessed or when they received adequate training."[41] Dobak may be correct, but the men of the USCT certainly neither were the first nor will be the last soldiers, black or white, to emerge less than heroic while charging an entrenched enemy.

Given the liabilities against the black soldiers, with enemies in their front and rear, the African Americans' performance in combat generally exceeded expectations. As a whole, the men of the USCT conducted themselves well as worthy representatives of Lincoln's government, according to one historian, "equal to, if not superior to, white southerners in bravery and skill."[42] They generally exhibited the same degrees of courage, loyalty, and resolve as white troops. A contemporary did not exaggerate when he wrote, "Their enthusiasm in this particular has no parallel in the history of the war."[43]

That said, Lincoln's military emancipation project depended largely on white Union troops to implement emancipation, and the president provided few guideposts for the newly freed men and women. His government provided no map, no plan for the former slaves to navigate white racism, to avail themselves of the opportunities and sidestep the challenges of freedom, especially in the defeated Confederate states. Though cut down before he could begin Reconstruction in earnest, in his last days Lincoln failed to provide any short-term protection for the freedmen's hard-won liberty.[44] Beyond this, no matter what Lincoln could say or do to advance the cause of the USCT, many whites, in the North and the South, judged the prospect of blacks in uniform infuriating. They often considered the men of the USCT disrespectful, incapable, and indolent. Whites, within and beyond the U.S. Army, frequently showered the black troops with racist slurs—sometimes even violent acts. In November 1863, for example, white Philadelphians mobbed the Second USCT as it boarded a troop train. Others stoned the cars as they wended their way northward.[45]

All told, Lincoln's decision to use military emancipation as a weapon to keep the nation together changed America in ways that neither he nor the African American soldiers could envision. Worried that the courts might overturn his emancipation order, in late 1863 Lincoln began the long process of passing a constitutional amendment to safeguard his emancipation decree from being nullified. Finally passing both houses of Congress on January 31, 1865, the new amendment, according to Lincoln, signified "a King's cure for all the evils" of slavery.[46] Three hundred nine days later, on December 6,

1865, three-quarters of the states ratified the Thirteenth Amendment. Lincoln of course had been dead for months.

With the Thirteenth Amendment ratified, racially based slavery no longer stained the fabric of American life. And during Reconstruction, blacks would gain (and then continue to fight to retain) citizenship rights and suffrage. Service in the USCT had enabled African Americans to begin the long journey upward to true freedom. Lincoln's military edict also enabled the men of the USCT to assert their collective manhood, the sense of their own worth. "By arming black men," J. Matthew Gallman explains, "the Union was acknowledging something about black humanity and specifically about the capacity of these men to serve in uniform."[47] Lincoln had served as both their emancipator and their enabler.

Military service enabled African Americans to participate in the revolutionary crusade of destroying slavery, reuniting the nation, gaining freedom, and earning the respect of many white soldiers and officers. Joining Lincoln's army enabled the men of the USCT to take revenge for centuries of bondage and proscription and also to begin laying the foundation for better lives for themselves and their families following the war. In the short term, military service enabled free blacks and slaves to obtain better food, shelter, and clothing. Though whites might continue to consider blacks their inferiors, during the Civil War men of color, nonetheless, had proven themselves most un-slavelike, capable of fighting like men. They had played an important role in defeating the Confederates.[48]

Lincoln may have conferred freedom on the slaves, but the black men proved their masculinity by their yeoman-like and at times intrepid service as soldiers. No longer slaves, they avowed their manhood by fighting and demanding respect as soldiers and as men. Military service translated during the war and for decades afterward as evidence of black accomplishment, earning for USCT veterans status as well as postwar victories large and small in civil and political affairs. They provided leadership in black communities nationally, including in struggles over citizenship, suffrage, and school and streetcar desegregation.[49] In June 1865, for example, freedmen in Norfolk, Virginia, agitated for equal rights, arguing that they had "fully proved their patriotism and possession of all the manly qualities that adorn the soldier."[50] As soldiers, the men of the USCT gained confidence and determination to join the body politic. Their opportunity to serve in the U.S. military empowered blacks as freedmen with expectations in the post-emancipation age. As Eric Foner observes, Lincoln believed that with their military service black men had "staked a claim to citizenship in the postwar nation."[51]

In May 1864, the *Black Warrior*, the camp newspaper of the all-black Fourteenth Rhode Island Heavy Artillery (Colored) (renamed the Eleventh U.S. Colored Heavy Artillery), made the connection that Lincoln had identified between military emancipation and preserving the American Republic. The newspaper's artillerist-editors informed their readers that "upon your prowess, discipline, and character; depend the destinies of four millions of people and the triumph of the principles of freedom and self government of this great republic." African Americans, of course, who gained freedom and the chance to fight their masters, never doubted that the war centered on slavery. God, black troops agreed, used the war to redeem the nation, to challenge racial inequality, and to reclaim black manhood. Service in the USCT afforded black men "independence, courage, the right to bear arms, moral agency, liberty of conscience, and the ability to protect and care for one's family." Private Robert Fitzgerald joined the Fifth Massachusetts Cavalry, he said, to "prove our Love of Liberty"—"that we be men." When a white man insulted one of Colonel Thomas Wentworth Higginson's men by asking him, "What are you, anyhow?" the soldier stood erect and replied, "When God made me, I wasn't much, but I's a man now."[52]

Emancipation and Federal military service put a human face on black Americans, who were now to be seen as men, no longer as property. "The [final] proclamation addressed slaves directly, not as the property of the country's enemies but as persons with wills of their own whose actions might help win the Civil War," Foner concludes. Their success earned them both the nation and Lincoln's appreciation for and understanding of "blacks' relationship to the nation."[53] In 1932 Andrew Evans, who had served as a private in the Seventeenth USCT, recalled: "Of course, we all decided that the only thing for us to do was to join the Union army and fight for the man who had done so much for us."[54]

His emancipation project not only empowered African Americans and changed America, but it also changed Abraham Lincoln. "It liberated him from his old dilemma (his hatred of slavery and his impotence to remove it where it existed) and enabled him to act more consistently with his moral convictions," writes Stephen B. Oates.[55] The revolution Lincoln sparked enabled the president to reconcile restoring the Union while retaining his commitment to decency, dignity, and justice for all people. And after another century of struggle, it finally allowed people of color to attain full American citizenship.

ACKNOWLEDGMENTS

My thanks go to Sylvia Frank Rodrigue, Sara Vaughn Gabbard, and Richard W. Etulain for inviting me to write this book. Their comments proved invaluable, as did those of an anonymous reader. Barbara Martin and Wayne Larsen of Southern Illinois University Press rallied to my support at a critical juncture, and Kathleen Kageff expertly copyedited the manuscript. Jane Henderson prepared the index. At the University of North Carolina at Charlotte, Leigh Robbins provided invaluable secretarial support. Amanda Binder, Ed Bradley, Eric Courtney, Ann Davis, Elizabeth Dunn, J. Matthew Gallman, James J. Harris, William C. Harris, Randall M. Miller, Jeff Shaara, Brooks D. Simpson, Lois Stickell, Daniel W. Stowell, and Peter Thorsheim assisted me with various aspects of my research. The late Walter B. Hill invited me in 1996 to serve on the Historian Advisory Committee, African American Civil War Memorial Foundation, Washington, D.C. I presented some of the material contained in this book at Lincoln Memorial University, Harrogate, Tennessee, in 2006, at the Universität Hamburg, Hamburg, Germany, in 2010, and at the John Brown Russwurm Lecture, Bowdoin College, in 2012. The University of North Carolina Press has graciously allowed me to adapt material that first appeared in my edited *Black Soldiers in Blue: African American Troops in the Civil War Era* (2002). Sylvia A. Smith waited patiently for me to complete another book. She knows what Abraham Lincoln "is doing." As for OLM, the dedication says it all.

NOTES

Introduction

1. Hannibal Cox, poem sent to Lincoln, March 30, 1864; Benjamin Woodward to Lincoln, April 11, 1864, Abraham Lincoln Papers, Manuscript Division, Library of Congress (hereafter LPLC).

2. Cox poem, LPLC.

3. Woodward to Lincoln, April 11, 1864, LPLC.

4. C. W. Foster to E. D. Townsend, October, 20, 1865, E. D. Townsend to Edwin M. Stanton, October 20, 1866, in U.S. War Department, *The War of the Rebellion: A Compilation of the Official Records of the Union and Confederate Armies*, 128 vols. (Washington, DC: Government Printing Office, 1880–1901), ser. 3, vol. 5, pp. 138, 1028; Dudley Taylor Cornish, *The Sable Arm: Negro Troops in the Union Army, 1861–1865* (1956; reprint, New York: W. W. Norton, 1966), 288; Ira Berlin, ed., *Freedom: A Documentary History of Emancipation, 1861–1867*. Ser. 2. *The Black Military Experience* (Cambridge: Cambridge University Press, 1982), 12, Table 1; Stephanie McCurry, *Confederate Reckoning: Power and Politics in the Civil War South* (Cambridge: Harvard University Press, 2010), 319; William A. Dobak, *Freedom by the Sword: The U.S. Colored Troops, 1862–1867* (Washington, DC: Center of Military History, U.S. Army, 2011), 504; Ira Berlin et al., eds., *Freedom: A Documentary History of Emancipation, 1861–1867*. Ser. 1, vol. 1. *The Destruction of Slavery* (Cambridge: Cambridge University Press, 1985), 37.

5. David Slay, "Abraham Lincoln and the United States Colored Troops of Mississippi," *Journal of Mississippi History* 70 (Spring 2008): 67–68, 85–86.

6. Arna Bontemps, *Free at Last: The Life of Frederick Douglass* (New York: Dodd, Mead, 1971), 224.

7. Lincoln to James C. Conkling, August 26, 1863, in Roy P. Basler, ed., *Collected Works of Abraham Lincoln*, 8 vols. (New Brunswick: Rutgers University Press, 1953), 6:409, 410 (hereafter *CW*).

8. Stephen B. Oates, "The Slaves Freed," *American Heritage* 32 (December 1980): 81.

9. Henry McNeal Turner, *The Negro in Slavery, War, and Peace* (1913), in James M. McPherson, *The Negro's Civil War: How American Negroes Felt and Acted during the War for the Union* (1965; reprint, Urbana: University of Illinois Press, 1982), 50.

10. Sean Wilentz, "Who Lincoln Was," *New Republic* 240, no. 12–13 (July 15, 2009): 35.

11. Allen C. Guelzo, *Fateful Lightning: A New History of the Civil War and Reconstruction* (New York: Oxford University Press, 2012), 541; Allen C. Guelzo, *Lincoln's Emancipation Proclamation: The End of Slavery in America* (New York: Simon and Schuster, 2004), 229.

12. "The War in Florida: Negro Troops against the Rebels," *New York Times*, February 10, 1863, p. 2; Thomas Wentworth Higginson, *Army Life in a Black Regiment* (1869; reprint, Boston: Beacon Press, 1962), 71.

13. Eric Foner, "The Ideology of the Republican Party," in Robert Engs and Randall M. Miller, eds., *The Birth of the Grand Old Party: The Republicans' First Generation* (Philadelphia: University of Pennsylvania Press, 2002), 11.

14. Michael Burlingame, *Lincoln and the Civil War* (Carbondale: Southern Illinois University Press, 2011), 88–89.

15. Lincoln to Michael Hahn, March 13, 1864, *CW*, 7:243.

16. Lincoln, Last Public Address, April 11, 1865, *CW*, 8:403.

17. William C. Davis, *Lincoln's Men: How President Lincoln Became Father to an Army and a Nation* (New York: Free Press, 1999), 164.

18. Peter J. Parish, *Abraham Lincoln and American Nationhood* (London: Institute of United States Studies, 2000), 13.

19. Lincoln, Interview with Alexander W. Randall and Joseph T. Mills, August 19, 1864, *CW*, 7:506–7.

20. James M. McPherson, *How Lincoln Won the War with Metaphors* (Fort Wayne: Louis A. Warren Lincoln Library and Museum, 1985), 19; Lincoln to Reverdy Johnson, July 26, 1862, *CW*, 5:343.

21. "Abe Lincoln's Last Card; Or, Rouge-et-Noir (Red and Black)," *Punch* 43 (October 18, 1862): 161.

22. Lincoln, Final Emancipation Proclamation, January 1, 1863, *CW*, 6:30.

23. Lincoln, Address at Sanitary Fair, Baltimore, Maryland, April 18, 1864, *CW*, 7:302.

24. Editorial, "Use of Negroes as Soldiers," *New York Times*, February 16, 1863, p. 4.

25. Charles L. Blockson, "A History of the Blackman in Montgomery County," *Bulletin of the Historical Society of Montgomery County* 18 (Spring 1973): 345.

26. Gregory J. W. Urwin, "Sowing the Wind and Reaping the Whirlwind: Abraham Lincoln as a War President," in Randall M. Miller, ed., *Lincoln and Leadership: Military, Political, and Religious Decision Making* (New York: Fordham University Press, 2012), 51.

27. Noah Andre Trudeau, *Like Men of War: Black Troops in the Civil War, 1862–1865* (Boston: Little, Brown, 1998), 466; Joseph A. Glatthaar, *Forged in Battle: The Civil War Alliance of Black Soldiers and White Officers* (New York: Free Press, 1990), 71, Appendix 2.

28. Joseph P. Reidy, "The African American Struggle for Citizenship Rights in the Northern States during the Civil War," in Susannah J. Ural, ed., *Civil War Citizens: Race, Ethnicity, and Identity in America's Bloodiest Conflict* (New York: New York University Press, 2010), 224.

29. Louis P. Masur, *Lincoln's Hundred Days: The Emancipation Proclamation and the War for the Union* (Cambridge: Belknap Press of Harvard University Press, 2012), 8–9.

1. The Final Emancipation Proclamation and Military Emancipation

1. Lincoln, Final Emancipation Proclamation, January 1, 1863, in Roy P. Basler, ed., *Collected Works of Abraham Lincoln*, 8 vols. (New Brunswick: Rutgers University Press, 1953), 6:29–30 (hereafter *CW*).

2. Theodore Tilton to Lincoln, telegram, February 3, 1863, Abraham Lincoln Papers, Manuscript Division, Library of Congress (hereafter LPLC).

3. Lincoln, Proclamation Calling Militia and Convening Congress, April 15, 1861, *CW*, 4:332; Frederick Douglass, "How to End the War" (May 1861), *Douglass' Monthly*, in Philip S. Foner, ed., *The Life and Writings of Frederick Douglass*, 5 vols. (New York: International Publishers, 1952–75), 3:94; James G. Fee, *Autobiography of John G. Fee, Berea, Kentucky* (Chicago: National Christian Association, 1891), 156–57.

4. *New York Express* in James M. McPherson, *The Struggle for Equality: Abolitionists and the Negro in the Civil War and Reconstruction* (1964; reprint, Princeton: Princeton University Press, 1995), 192, 194.

5. La Wanda Cox, *Lincoln and Black Freedom: A Study in Presidential Leadership* (Columbia: University of South Carolina Press, 1981), 23.

6. Mark E. Neely Jr., *The Last Best Hope of Earth: Abraham Lincoln and the Promise of America* (Cambridge: Harvard University Press, 1993), 100–101, 103; Ira Berlin, ed., *Freedom: A Documentary History of Emancipation, 1861–1867.* Ser. 2. *The Black Military Experience* (Cambridge: Cambridge University Press, 1982), 3–4.

7. Lincoln to Cuthbert Bullitt, July 28, 1862, *CW*, 5:345.

8. Ira Berlin, "Emancipation and Its Meaning," in David W. Blight and Brooks D. Simpson, eds., *Union and Emancipation: Essays on Politics and Race in the Civil War Era* (Kent: Kent State University Press, 1997), 110–11; James M. McPherson, "Who Freed the Slaves?" *Reconstruction* 2 (1994): 40.

9. "An Act to Confiscate Property Used for Insurrectionary Purposes," August 6, 1861, in U.S. Congress, *The Statutes at Large, Treaties, and Proclamations of the United States of America*, 111 vols. to date (Boston: Little, Brown, 1863–), 12:319; John Syrett, "The Confiscation Acts: Efforts at Reconstruction during the Civil War" (Ph.D., diss., University of

Wisconsin, 1971), chapter 1; J. Matthew Gallman, *The North Fights the Civil War: The Home Front* (Chicago: Ivan R. Dee, 1994), 132; James M. McPherson, *Ordeal by Fire: The Civil War and Reconstruction* (New York: Alfred A. Knopf, 1982), 267.

10. Silvana R. Siddali, *From Property to Person: Slavery and the Confiscation Acts, 1861–1862* (Baton Rouge: Louisiana State University Press, 2005), 91.

11. James G. Randall, *Constitutional Problems under Lincoln*, rev. ed. (1951; reprint, Urbana: University of Illinois Press, 1964), 276, 357; Lincoln to Orville H. Browning, September 22, 1861, *CW*, 4:532; Parker Pillsbury (February 15, 1862) in Stacey M. Robertson, *Parker Pillsbury: Radical Abolitionist, Male Feminist* (Ithaca: Cornell University Press, 2000), 123.

12. Thomas A. Scott to Thomas W. Sherman, October 14, 1861, in U.S. War Department, *The War of the Rebellion: A Compilation of the Official Records of the Union and Confederate Armies*, 128 vols. (Washington, DC: Government Printing Office, 1880–1901), ser. 1, vol. 1, pp. 176–77 (hereafter *OR*).

13. Draft and final versions of Cameron's annual report appear in Edward McPherson, *The Political History of the United States of America during the Great Rebellion, 1860–1865*, 2nd ed. (1865; reprint, New York: Da Capo Press, 1972), 249.

14. Lincoln to Albert G. Hodges, April 4, 1864, *CW*, 7:281–82; Hans L. Trefousse, *Thaddeus Stevens: Nineteenth-Century Egalitarian* (Chapel Hill: University of North Carolina Press, 1997), 116; David Donald, *Charles Sumner & The Rights of Man* (New York: Alfred A. Knopf, 1970), 48; Edward Magdol, *Owen Lovejoy: Abolitionist in Congress* (New Brunswick: Rutgers University Press, 1967), 300; Bruce Tap, *Over Lincoln's Shoulder: The Committee on the Conduct of the War* (Lawrence: University Press of Kansas, 1998), 19.

15. Dudley Taylor Cornish, *The Sable Arm: Negro Troops in the Union Army, 1861–1865* (1956; reprint, New York: W. W. Norton, 1966), 72–78.

16. John W. Phelps to R. S. Davis, July 30, 1862, in Berlin, ed., *The Black Military Experience*, 62.

17. Ibid., 43, 44, 63n; John W. Phelps to Benjamin F. Butler, August 2, 1862, in Berlin, ed., *The Black Military Experience*, 63–65, 65n; Excerpt of testimony of General B. F. Butler [May 1, 1863], in Berlin, ed., *The Black Military Experience*, 312, 315n; Richard J. Sommers, *Richmond Redeemed: The Siege of Petersburg* (Garden City: Doubleday, 1981), 31; Edward G. Longacre, "Black Troops in the Army of the James, 1863–65," *Military Affairs* 45 (February 1981): 1.

18. Edward A. Miller Jr., *Lincoln's Abolitionist General: The Biography of David Hunter* (Columbia: University of South Carolina Press, 1997), 96–102.

19. Carl Schurz to Lincoln, Friday, May 16, 1862, LPLC; Phillip S. Paludan, "Greeley, Colonization, and a 'Deputation of Negroes,'" in Brian R. Dirck, ed., *Lincoln Emancipated: The President and the Politics of Race* (DeKalb: Northern Illinois University Press, 2007), 40.

20. Lincoln, Proclamation Revoking General Hunter's Order of Military Emancipation of May 9, 1862, May 19, 1862, *CW*, 5:222–23.

21. Eric Foner, *The Fiery Trial: Abraham Lincoln and American Slavery* (New York: W. W. Norton, 2010), 207.

22. Berlin, ed., *The Black Military Experience*, 37–39; McPherson, *The Struggle for Equality*, 195–96; Lincoln to Albert G. Hodges, April 4, 1864, *CW*, 7:282; Norwood P. Hallowell, *The Negro as a Soldier in the War of the Rebellion* (Boston: Little, Brown, 1897), 4.

23. Stephen V. Ash, *Firebrand of Liberty: The Story of Two Black Regiments That Changed the Course of the Civil War* (New York: W. W. Norton, 2008), 33.

24. John M. Hawks, "The First Freedmen to Become Soldiers," *Southern Workman* 38 (January 1909): 108; *New York Herald*, August 6, 1862, in Charles M. Segal, ed., *Conversations with Lincoln* (New York: G. P. Putnam's Sons, 1961), 187; [Charles W. Wills], *Army Life of an Illinois Soldier* (Washington, DC: Globe Printing Company, 1906), 125; Lincoln, Remarks to a Deputation of Western Gentlemen, August 4, 1862, and Lincoln, Reply to Emancipation Memorial Presented by Chicago Christians of All Denominations, September 13, 1862, *CW*, 5:356–57, 423.

25. Edwin M. Stanton to Rufus Saxton, August 25, 1862, *OR*, ser. 1, vol. 14, pp. 377–78; Berlin, ed., *The Black Military Experience*, 39–41; William L. Garrison to Fanny Garrison, September 25, 1862, in Walter M. Merrill and Louis Ruchames, eds., *The Letters of William Lloyd Garrison*, 6 vols. (Cambridge: Harvard University Press, 1971–81), 5:114–15.

26. John E. Johns, *Florida during the Civil War* (Gainesville: University of Florida Press, 1963), 153.

27. Charles A. Wickliffe and Robert Mallory (July 5, 1862) in *Congressional Globe*, July 8, 1862, Thirty-Seventh Congress, Second Session (Washington, DC: Congressional Globe Office, 1862), 3123–24, 3127.

28. Stevens (July 5, 1862) in *Congressional Globe*, July 8, 1862, 3127, 3125, 3126, 3127.

29. Lincoln, Drafts of a Bill for Compensated Emancipation in Delaware, [November 26? 1861], *CW*, 5:29–30.

30. Lincoln, Annual Message to Congress, December 3, 1861, *CW*, 5:48–49.

31. Stephen B. Oates, "The Slaves Freed," *American Heritage* 32 (December 1980): 78.

32. Lincoln, Message to Congress, March 6, 1862, *CW*, 5:144–46; William E. Gienapp, "Abraham Lincoln and the Border States," *Journal of the Abraham Lincoln Association* 13 (1992): 33.

33. Lincoln, Proclamation Revoking General Hunter's Order of Military Emancipation of May 9, 1862, May 19, 1862, *CW*, 5:223.

34. "An Act to Make an Additional Article of War," March 13, 1862, in U.S. Congress, *The Statutes at Large*, 12:354.

35. Lincoln, Message to Congress, April 16, 1862, *CW*, 5:192.

36. "An Act to Secure Freedom to all Persons within the Territories of the United States," June 19, 1862, in U.S. Congress, *The Statutes at Large*, 12:432.

37. Lincoln, Appeal to Border State Representatives to Favor Compensated Emancipation, July 12, 1862, *CW*, 5:318.

38. Michael Vorenberg, "Abraham Lincoln and the Politics of Black Colonization," *Journal of the Abraham Lincoln Association* 14 (1993): 24, 40, 44.

39. Lincoln, Annual Message to Congress, December 3, 1861, *CW*, 5:48.

40. Charles H. Wesley, "The Struggle for the Recognition of Haiti and Liberia as Independent Republics," *Journal of Negro History* 2 (October 1917): 369–83.

41. Glenn David Brasher, *The Peninsula Campaign and the Necessity of Emancipation: African Americans and the Fight for Freedom* (Chapel Hill: University of North Carolina Press, 2012), 74, 189, 214.

42. "An Act to Amend the Act Calling Forth the Militia to Execute the Laws of the Union, Suppress Insurrections, and Repel Invasions," July 17, 1862, in U.S. Congress, *The Statutes at Large*, 12:599.

43. Herman Belz, "Race, Law, and Politics in the Struggle for Equal Pay during the Civil War," *Civil War History* 22 (September 1976): 210–11.

44. Frederick Douglass, "The Slaveholders' Rebellion" (August 1862) and "The President and His Speeches" (September 1862), *Douglass' Monthly*, in Foner, ed., *The Life and Writings of Frederick Douglass*, 3:256, 268–69.

45. "An Act to Suppress Insurrection, to Punish Treason and Rebellion, to Seize and Confiscate the Property of Rebels, and for Other Purposes," July 17, 1862, in U.S. Congress, *The Statutes at Large*, 12:589–92.

46. "Colored Regiments," *Oberlin Evangelist* 4 (July 16, 1862): 116.

47. Editorial, (San Francisco) *Pacific Appeal* 1 (July 19, 1862): 2.

48. Siddali, *From Property to Person*, 229.

49. Daniel W. Hamilton, *The Limits of Sovereignty: Property Confiscation in the Union and the Confederacy during the Civil War* (Chicago: University of Chicago Press, 2007), 141.

50. Matthew Pinsker, "Lincoln's Summer of Emancipation," in Harold Holzer and Sara Vaughn Gabbard, eds., *Lincoln and Freedom: Slavery, Emancipation, and the Thirteenth Amendment* (Carbondale: Southern Illinois University Press, 2007), 80–81; Elizabeth D. Leonard, *Lincoln's Forgotten Ally: Judge Advocate General Joseph Holt of Kentucky* (Chapel Hill: University of North Carolina Press, 2011), 161.

51. Foner, *The Fiery Trial*, 218.

52. Salmon P. Chase, July 22, 1862, in David Donald, ed., *Inside Lincoln's Cabinet: The Civil War Diaries of Salmon P. Chase* (New York: Longmans, Green, 1954), 99. For the draft, see Lincoln, Emancipation Proclamation—First Draft [July 22, 1862], *CW*, 5:336–37.

53. Lincoln, Memorandum on Recruiting Negroes [July 22, 1862?], *CW*, 5:338 (emphasis in original).

54. John T. Hubbell, "Abraham Lincoln and the Recruitment of Black Soldiers," *Journal of the Abraham Lincoln Association* 2 (1980): 11; Oates, "The Slaves Freed," 81.

55. Lincoln, Annual Message to Congress, December 1, 1862, *CW*, 5:530–31.

56. Salmon P. Chase to Lincoln, December 31, 1862, LPLC.

57. Lincoln to Albert G. Hodges, April 4, 1864, *CW*, 7:282; Joseph T. Glatthaar, "Black Glory: The African-American Role in Union Victory," in Gabor S. Boritt, ed., *Why the Confederacy Lost* (New York: Oxford University Press, 1992), 142.

58. Frederick Douglass, "The Reasons for Our Troubles" (February 1862) and "The Proclamation and a Negro Army" (March 1863), *Douglass' Monthly*, in Foner, ed., *The Life and Writings of Frederick Douglass*, 3:204, 322.

59. John White Geary to Mary, September 25, 1862, in William Alan Blair, ed., *A Politician Goes to War: The Civil War Letters of John White Geary* (University Park: Pennsylvania State University Press, 1995), 56; John Quincy Adams Campbell, September 25 [1862], in Mark Grimsley and Todd D. Miller, eds., *The Union Must Stand: The Civil War Diary of John Quincy Adams Campbell, Fifth Iowa Volunteer Infantry* (Knoxville: University of Tennessee Press, 2000), 61; George H. Boker, *Washington and Jackson on Negro Soldiers. Gen. Banks on the Bravery of Negro Troops. Poem—the Second Louisiana* (Philadelphia: Printed for Gratuitous Distribution [n.p., 1863]), 15.

60. Andrew Ward, *River Run Red: The Fort Pillow Massacre in the American Civil War* (New York: Viking, 2005), 6.

61. Foner, *The Fiery Trial*, 241–42.

62. Howard C. Westwood, "Lincoln's Position on Black Enlistments," in *Black Troops, White Commanders, and Freedmen during the Civil War* (Carbondale: Southern Illinois University Press, 1992), 15; Michael Vorenberg, *Final Freedom: The Civil War, the Abolition of Slavery, and the Thirteenth Amendment* (Cambridge: Cambridge University Press, 2001), 25; George M. Fredrickson, *The Inner Civil War: Northern Intellectuals and the Crisis of the Union* (New York: Harper and Row, 1965), 120.

63. William Lloyd Garrison to Fanny Garrison, September 25, 1862, in Merrill and Ruchames, eds., *The Letters of William Lloyd Garrison*, 5:114; Moncure Conway in John d'Tremont, *Southern Emancipator: Moncure*

Conway: The American Years, 1832–1865 (New York: Oxford University Press, 1987), 180.

64. George E. Stephens to the editor, December 31, 1862, in *New York Weekly Anglo-African*, January 17, 1863, in Donald Yacovone, ed., *A Voice of Thunder: The Civil War Letters of George E. Stephens* (Urbana: University of Illinois Press, 1997), 219.

65. Brian Taylor, "A Politics of Service: Black Northerners' Debates over Enlistment in the American Civil War," *Civil War History* 58 (December 2012): 454, 480.

66. Stephens to the editor, May 26, August 1, 1864, in *New York Weekly Anglo-African*, June 18, September 3, 1864, in Yacovone, ed., *A Voice of Thunder*, 306, 324.

67. Joseph T. Wilson, *The Black Phalanx: African American Soldiers in the War of Independence, the War of 1812, and the Civil War* (1887; reprint, New York: Da Capo Press, 1994), 200; Kirkwood to Henry W. Halleck, August 5, 1862, in Berlin, ed., *The Black Military Experience*, 85.

68. Charles Francis Adams Jr., to father, November 2, 1864, to Henry Adams, April 6, 1862, to father, July 28, 1862, in Worthington Chauncey Ford, ed., *A Cycle of Adams Letters, 1861–1865*, 2 vols. (Boston: Houghton Mifflin, 1920), 2:215; 1:131, 171 (emphasis in original).

69. George Washington Williams, *A History of the Negro Troops in the War of the Rebellion, 1861–1865* (1887; reprint, New York: Fordham University Press, 2012), 120, 127.

70. George Washington Whitman to mother, September 30, 1862, in Jerome M. Loving, ed., *Civil War Letters of George Washington Whitman* (Durham: Duke University Press, 1975), 71; Squier to Ellen, December 24, 1862, in Julie A. Doyle, John David Smith, and Richard M. McMurry, eds., *This Wilderness of War: The Civil War Letters of George W. Squier, Hoosier Volunteer* (Knoxville: University of Tennessee Press, 1998), 30.

71. Henry Livermore Abbott to Aunt Lizzie, January 10, 1863, in Robert Garth Scott, ed., *Fallen Leaves: The Civil War Letters of Major Henry Livermore Abbott* (Kent: Kent State University Press, 1991), 18; John J. Hennessy, ed., *Fighting with the Eighteenth Massachusetts: The Civil War Memoir of Thomas H. Mann* (Baton Rouge: Louisiana State University Press, 2000), 142; Felix Brannigan in Benjamin Quarles, *The Negro in the Civil War* (1953; reprint, Boston: Little, Brown, 1969), 31.

72. Symmes Stillwell and William C. H. Reeder in James M. McPherson, *For Cause and Comrades: Why Men Fought in the Civil War* (New York: Oxford University Press, 1997), 126, 128–29; Henry Phelps Hubbell to Walter S. Hubbell, January 26, 1863, in Simon P. Newman, "A Democrat in Lincoln's Army: The Civil War Letters of Henry P. Hubbell," *Princeton University Library Chronicle* 50, no. 2 (1989): 163–64.

73. Lincoln to William T. Sherman, July 18, 1864, *CW*, 7:449–50; William T. Sherman to William M. McPherson [c. September 15–30, 1864], in Brooks D. Simpson and Jean V. Berlin, eds., *Sherman's Civil War: Selected Correspondence of William T. Sherman, 1860–1865* (Chapel Hill: University of North Carolina Press, 1999), 727; William T. Sherman to Henry W. Halleck, January 12, 1865, *OR*, ser. 1, vol. 47, pt. 2, p. 37.

74. Lincoln to James C. Conkling, August 26, 1863, *CW*, 6:408n9.

75. Thomas Wentworth Higginson, "Scattered Notes about T.W.H.'s Colored Troops, 1864," in Christopher Looby, ed., *The Complete Civil War Journal and Selected Letters of Thomas Wentworth Higginson* (Chicago: University of Chicago Press, 2000), 1; anonymous soldier to Edwin M. Stanton, October 2, 1865, in Berlin, ed., *The Black Military Experience*, 654; Robert Scott Davis Jr., "A Soldier's Story: The Records of Hubbard Pryor, Forty-Fourth United States Colored Troops," *Prologue* 31 (Winter 1999): 267–68, 270.

76. Frederick Douglass, "Emancipation Proclaimed" (October 1862), *Douglass' Monthly*, in Foner, ed., *The Life and Writings of Frederick Douglass*, 3:276.

2. Emancipation and Mobilization

1. William C. Davis, *Lincoln's Men: How President Lincoln Became Father to an Army and a Nation* (New York: Free Press, 1999), 157.

2. Randall M. Miller in John Van Horne, ed., *Phil Lapsansky: Appreciations, A Collection of Essays Honoring Phillip S. Lapsansky on His Retirement after More than Forty Years of Service to the Library Company of Philadelphia, 1971–2012* (Philadelphia: Library Company of Philadelphia, 2012), 100.

3. Henry Carey Baird, *General Washington and General Jackson on Negro Soldiers* (Philadelphia: Henry Carey Baird, 1863), 8.

4. Frederick Douglass, "Condition of the Country" (February 1863), *Douglass' Monthly*, in Philip S. Foner, ed., *The Life and Writings of Frederick Douglass*, 5 vols. (New York: International Publishers, 1952–75), 3:317; Lincoln to Nathaniel P. Banks, March 29, 1863, to Andrew Johnson, March 26, 1863, in Roy P. Basler, ed., *Collected Works of Abraham Lincoln*, 8 vols. (New Brunswick: Rutgers University Press, 1953), 6:154, 149–50 (hereafter *CW*).

5. Lincoln to Johnson, September 11, 1863, Abraham Lincoln Papers, Manuscript Division, Library of Congress (hereafter LPLC).

6. Lincoln, Remarks to New York Committee, May 30, 1863, *CW*, 6:239.

7. Lincoln to James C. Conkling, August 26, 1863, *CW*, 409.

8. *CW*, 6:408–9, 410; Lincoln, Address at Sanitary Fair, Baltimore, Maryland, April 18, 1864, *CW*, 7:302.

9. John Mercer Langston, *From the Virginia Plantation to the National Capitol: An Autobiography* (1894; reprint, New York: Berg Publishers, 1969), 206.

10. Gideon Welles, January 10, 1863, in Howard K. Beale, ed., *Diary of Gideon Welles: Secretary of the Navy Under Lincoln and Johnson*, 2 vols. (New York: W. W. Norton, 1960), 1:218.

11. Eric Foner, *The Fiery Trial: Abraham Lincoln and American Slavery* (New York: W. W. Norton, 2010), 250; Allen C. Guelzo, *Lincoln's Emancipation Proclamation: The End of Slavery in America* (New York: Simon and Schuster, 2004), 113, 116–17.

12. "An Act for enrolling and calling out the national Forces, and for other Purposes," March 3, 1863, in *The Statutes at Large, Treaties, and Proclamations of the United States of America*, 111 vols. to date (Boston: Little, Brown, 1863–), 12:731–37.

13. Ira Berlin, ed., *Freedom: A Documentary History of Emancipation, 1861–1867*. Ser. 2. *The Black Military Experience* (Cambridge: Cambridge University Press, 1982), 9–10; Frederick Douglass, "Men of Color, To Arms!" broadside (March 21, 1863), in Foner, ed., *The Life and Writings of Frederick Douglass*, 3:318.

14. John T. Hubbell, "Abraham Lincoln and the Recruitment of Black Soldiers," *Journal of the Abraham Lincoln Association* 2 (1980): 17.

15. Edwin M. Stanton to Lorenzo Thomas, March 25, 1863, in U.S. War Department, *The War of the Rebellion: A Compilation of the Official Records of the Union and Confederate Armies*, 128 vols. (Washington, DC: Government Printing Office, 1880–1901), ser. 3, vol. 3, p. 101 (hereafter *OR*); William A. Dobak, *Freedom by the Sword: The U.S. Colored Troops, 1862–1867* (Washington, DC: Center of Military History, U.S. Army, 2011), 167.

16. Sam Evans to Andrew Evans, May 10, June 14, 22, 1863, in Robert F. Engs and Corey M. Brooks, eds., *Their Patriotic Duty: The Civil War Letters of the Evans Family of Brown County, Ohio* (New York: Fordham University Press, 2007), 139, 158, 161; Dudley Taylor Cornish, *The Sable Arm: Negro Troops in the Union Army, 1861–1865* (1956; reprint, New York: W. W. Norton, 1966), 111.

17. Lincoln to Ulysses S. Grant, August 9, 1863, *CW*, 6:374.

18. Ulysses S. Grant to Lincoln, August 23, 1863, LPLC.

19. Ulysses S. Grant to Marcellus M. Crocker, August 28, 1863, in John Y. Simon, ed., *The Papers of Ulysses S. Grant*, 32 vols. (Carbondale: Southern Illinois University Press, 1967–2012), 9:208.

20. Cornish, *The Sable Arm*, 111, 114, 117–25; James B. Fry to Edwin M. Stanton, March 17, 1866, *OR*, ser 3., vol. 5, p. 660.

21. Foner, *The Fiery Trial*, 252.

22. William C. Harris, *Lincoln and the Border States: Preserving the Union* (Lawrence: University Press of Kansas, 2011), 270–73.

23. Lincoln to Robert C. Schenck, October 21, 1863, *CW*, 6:530.

24. John Hay, October 22, 1863, in Michael Burlingame, ed., *Inside Lincoln's White House: The Complete Civil War Diary of John Hay* (Carbondale: Southern Illinois University Press, 1997), 97.

25. John David Smith, "The Recruitment of Negro Soldiers in Kentucky, 1863–1865," *Register of the Kentucky Historical Society* 72 (October 1974): 364–90; Richard D. Sears, *Camp Nelson, Kentucky: A Civil War History* (Lexington: University Press of Kentucky, 2002), xxxvi.

26. Harris, *Lincoln and the Border States*, 243.

27. Aaron Astor, *Rebels on the Border: Civil War, Emancipation, and the Reconstruction of Kentucky and Missouri* (Baton Rouge: Louisiana State University Press, 2012), 132.

28. Sears, *Camp Nelson, Kentucky*, xxxvi.

29. Marion B. Lucas, "Freedom Is Better Than Slavery: Black Families and Soldiers in Civil War Kentucky," in Kent T. Dollar, Larry H. Whiteaker, and W. Calvin Dickinson, eds., *Sister States, Enemy States: The Civil War in Kentucky and Tennessee* (Lexington: University Press of Kentucky, 2009), 192.

30. Carrie H. Purnell to Lincoln, January 30, 1864, LPLC.

31. Harris, *Lincoln and the Border States*, 228; Lincoln to Edwin M. Stanton, July 21, 1863, Lincoln to Ulysses S. Grant, August 9, 1863, *CW*, 6:342, 374–75.

32. Thomas E. Bramlette to Lincoln, October 19, 1863, LPLC.

33. Harris, *Lincoln and the Border States*, 237.

34. Lucas, "Freedom Is Better Than Slavery," 193.

35. Thomas E. Bramlette to Lincoln, February 1, 1864, LPLC; Harris, *Lincoln and the Border States*, 237.

36. Harris, *Lincoln and the Border States*, 381n47; Lowell H. Harrison, *Lincoln of Kentucky* (Lexington: University Press of Kentucky, 2000), 183; Darrel E. Bigham, *On Jordan's Banks: Emancipation and Its Aftermath in the Ohio River Valley* (Lexington: University Press of Kentucky, 2006), 69.

37. Thomas E. Bramlette to Lincoln, March 8, 1864, LPLC (emphasis in original).

38. Harrison, *Lincoln of Kentucky*, 184.

39. J. A. Jacobs to Lincoln, March 13, 1864, *OR*, ser. 3, vol. 4, p. 176.

40. Harris, *Lincoln and the Border States*, 238–39; Harrison, *Lincoln of Kentucky*, 184.

41. Lincoln to Edwin M. Stanton, March 28, 1864, LPLC.

42. Lincoln to Albert G. Hodges, April 4, 1864, *CW*, 7:281–82; Harris, *Lincoln and the Border States*, 239–40.

43. Bigham, *On Jordan's Banks*, 70–71, 72; Sears, *Camp Nelson, Kentucky*, xxxv–xxxviii.

44. Augustus L. Chetlain, *Recollections of Seventy Years* (Galena, IL.: Gazette Publishing, 1899), 104.

45. Lincoln to Lorenzo Thomas, June 13, 1864, *CW*, 7:390.

46. Lincoln to John Glenn, February 7, 1865, *CW*, 8:266.

47. Lincoln to Edwin M. Stanton, February [7?], 1865, *CW*, 268.

48. Lorenzo Thomas to Lincoln, June 13, 1864, LPLC.

49. Thomas E. Bramlette to Lincoln, September 3, 1864, in Ira Berlin et al., eds., *Freedom: A Documentary History of Emancipation, 1861–1867.* Ser. 1, vol. 1. *The Destruction of Slavery* (Cambridge: Cambridge University Press, 1985), 604–6.

50. John M. Palmer, *Personal Recollections of John M. Palmer: The Story of an Earnest Life* (Cincinnati: Robert Clarke, 1901), 225.

51. Harris, *Lincoln and the Border States*, 264.

52. Ibid., 242; Ira Berlin et al., eds., *Freedom's Soldiers: The Black Military Experience in the Civil War* (Cambridge: Cambridge University Press, 1998), 16–17.

53. Edward Bates, May 16, 1863, in Howard K. Beale, ed., *The Diary of Edward Bates, 1859–1866* (Washington, DC: Government Printing Office, 1933), 292; Whitelaw Reid, "How Philadelphia Raises Negro Soldiers," June 22, 1863, in James G. Smart, ed., *A Radical View: The "Agate" Dispatches of Whitelaw Reid, 1861–1865*, 2 vols. (Memphis: Memphis State University Press, 1976), 2:97.

54. General Orders No. 143, May 22, 1863, Orders and Circulars, 1797–1910; Records of the Adjutant General's Office, 1780's–1917, Record Group 94, National Archives and Records Administration, Washington, DC.

55. J. Matthew Gallman, "Snapshots: Images of Men in the United States Colored Troops," *American Nineteenth Century History* 12, no. 2 (2012): 132.

56. Jeffry D. Wert, "Camp William Penn and the Black Soldier," *Pennsylvania History* 46 (October 1979): 338–39.

57. Joseph B. Ross, comp., *Tabular Analysis of the Records of the U.S. Colored Troops and Their Predecessor Units in the National Archives of the United States* (Washington, DC: National Archives and Records Service, 1973), 1, 8, 11, 27; Cornish, *The Sable Arm*, 130, 131.

58. "Manifesto of the Colored Citizens of the State of New York, July 16, 1863," in C. Peter Ripley, ed., *The Black Abolitionist Papers*, 5 vols. (Chapel Hill: University of North Carolina Press, 1985–92): 5:228.

59. Douglass, "Address for the Promotion of Colored Enlistments" (August 1863), *Douglass' Monthly*, in Foner, ed., *The Life and Writings of Frederick Douglass*, 3:365.

60. James Oakes, *The Radical and The Republican: Frederick Douglass, Abraham Lincoln, and the Triumph of Antislavery Politics* (New York: W. W. Norton, 2007), 230–32.

61. Norwood P. Hallowell, *The Negro as a Soldier in the War of the Rebellion* (Boston: Little, Brown, 1897), 7.

62. William R. Forstchen, "The 28th United States Colored Troops: Indiana's African-Americans Go to War, 1863–1865" (Ph.D. diss., Purdue University, 1994), 175.

63. Hallowell, *The Negro as a Soldier in the War of the Rebellion*, 7, 8, 9.

64. Ibid., 9, 10, 11.

65. Stephen V. Ash, *Firebrand of Liberty: The Story of Two Black Regiments That Changed the Course of the Civil War* (New York: W. W. Norton, 2008), 35.

66. Berlin, ed., *The Black Military Experience*, 434.

67. Christian G. Samito, *Becoming American under Fire: Irish Americans, African Americans, and the Politics of Citizenship during the Civil War Era* (Ithaca: Cornell University Press, 2009), 63.

68. Henry M. Turner to Robert S. Davis, October 13, 1864, in Simon, ed., *The Papers of Ulysses S. Grant*, 12:461–63.

69. Martin R. Delany in Frank [Frances] A. Rollin, *Life and Public Services of Martin R. Delany, Sub-assistant Commissioner Bureau Relief of Refugees, Freedmen, and of Abandoned Lands, and Late Major 104th U.S. Colored Troops* (Boston: Lee and Shepard, 1883), 167.

70. Philadelphia (Pa.) Supervisory Committee for Recruiting Colored Regiments, *Free Military School for Applicants for Commands of Colored Troops* (Philadelphia: King and Baird, Printers, 1863), 3, 12.

71. Nathan W. Daniels, March 26, 29, 1863, in C. P. Weaver, ed., *Thank God My Regiment an African One: The Civil War Diary of Colonel Nathan W. Daniels* (Baton Rouge: Louisiana State University Press, 1998), 64, 68.

72. Joseph A. Glatthaar, *Forged in Battle: The Civil War Alliance of Black Soldiers and White Officers* (New York: Free Press, 1990), 53; Gregory J. W. Urwin, "United States Colored Troops," in David S. Heidler and Jeanne T. Heidler, eds., *Encyclopedia of the American Civil War: A Political, Social, and Military History* (New York: W. W. Norton, 2000), 2002.

73. Cornish, *The Sable Arm*, 213, 288; Glatthaar, *Forged in Battle*, 53, 21; Dudley Taylor Cornish, "African American Troops in the Union Army," in Richard N. Current, ed., *Encyclopedia of the Confederacy*, 4 vols. (New York: Simon and Schuster, 1993), 1:10, 12.

74. Andrew Evans to Sam Evans, May 18, June 7, 1863; Sam Evans to Andrew Evans, June 1, 1863; Sam Evans to Amos A. Evans, June 9, 1863, in Engs and Brooks, eds., *Their Patriotic Duty*, 143, 153, 151, 155–56.

75. Dobak, *Freedom by the Sword*, 172–73.

3. Discrimination Front and Rear

1. George Washington Williams, *A History of the Negro Troops in the War of the Rebellion, 1861–1865* (1887; reprint, New York: Fordham University Press, 2012), 180; Whitelaw Reid, "How Not to Get Negro Soldiers," April 2, 1863, in James G. Smart, ed., *A Radical View: The "Agate" Dispatches of Whitelaw Reid, 1861–1865*, 2 vols. (Memphis: Memphis State University Press, 1976), 2:94, 95; James Henry Gooding in *New Bedford Mercury*, May 26, 1863, in Virginia M. Adams, ed., *On the Altar of Freedom: A Black Soldier's Civil War Letters from the Front* (Amherst: University of Massachusetts Press, 1991), 24; anonymous soldier to Edwin M. Stanton, October 2, 1865, in Ira Berlin, ed., *Freedom: A Documentary History of Emancipation, 1861–1867.* Ser. 2. *The Black Military Experience* (Cambridge: Cambridge University Press, 1982), 654.

2. Lincoln, "Emancipation Proclamation," January 1, 1863, in Roy P. Basler, ed., *Collected Works of Abraham Lincoln*, 8 vols. (New Brunswick: Rutgers University Press, 1953), 6:30 (hereafter *CW*).

3. John H. Westervelt, September 29, [1863], in Anita Palladino, ed., *Diary of a Yankee Engineer: The Civil War Story of John H. Westervelt, Engineer, 1st New York Volunteer Engineer Corps* (New York: Fordham University Press, 1997), 43, 44.

4. [Nimrod Rowley] to the president, [August], 1864, in Berlin ed., *The Black Military Experience*, 501; Thomas D. Freeman in Susan-Mary Grant, "Fighting for Freedom: African-American Soldiers in the Civil War," in Susan-Mary Grant and Brian Holden Reid, eds., *The American Civil War: Explorations and Reconsiderations* (Harlow, England: Pearson Education, 2000), 205.

5. General Orders No. 21, June 14, 1864, in Berlin, ed., *The Black Military Experience*, 500–501, 487n; William T. Sherman to John A. Spooner, July 30, 1864, in Brooks D. Simpson and Jean V. Berlin, eds., *Sherman's Civil War: Selected Correspondence of William T. Sherman, 1860–1865* (Chapel Hill: University of North Carolina Press, 1999), 678.

6. Dudley Taylor Cornish, *The Sable Arm: Negro Troops in the Union Army, 1861–1865* (1956; reprint, New York: W. W. Norton, 1966), 288; Berlin, ed., *The Black Military Experience*, 633; James M. McPherson, *Ordeal by Fire: The Civil War and Reconstruction* (New York: Alfred A. Knopf, 1982), 354; Joseph A. Glatthaar, *Forged in Battle: The Civil War Alliance of Black Soldiers and White Officers* (New York: Free Press, 1990), 194–95, 190–91; Margaret Humphreys, *Intensely Human: The Health of the Black Soldiers in the American Civil War* (Baltimore: Johns Hopkins University Press, 2008), 11.

7. Grant, "Fighting for Freedom," 203; Versalle F. Washington, *Eagles on Their Buttons: A Black Infantry Regiment in the Civil War* (Columbia: University of Missouri Press, 1999), 32–33; Berlin, ed., *The Black Military Experience*, 634–35; John H. Westervelt, September 29, 1863, in Palladino, ed., *Diary of a Yankee Engineer*, 44; James M. Paradis, *Strike the Blow for Freedom: The 6th United States Colored Infantry in the Civil War* (Shippensburg, PA: White Mane Books, 1998), 15–16.

8. William A. Gladstone, *United States Colored Troops, 1863–1867* (Gettysburg: Thomas Publications, 1990), 72, 73; Norwood P. Hallowell, *The Negro as a Soldier in the War of the Rebellion* (Boston: Little, Brown, 1897), 23; Glatthaar, *Forged in Battle*, 185–86; [Edward W. Hinks] to Benjamin F. Butler, April 29, 1864, in Berlin, ed., *The Black Military Experience*, 548, 549; Edward W. Bacon to father, January 6, 1865, in George S. Burkhardt, ed., *Double Duty in the Civil War: The Letters of Sailor and Soldier Edward W. Bacon* (Carbondale: Southern Illinois University Press, 2009), 142.

9. John Cimprich and Robert C. Mainfort Jr., eds., "Fort Pillow Revisited: New Evidence about an Old Controversy," *Civil War History* 28 (December 1982): 295; Joseph T. Wilson, *The Black Phalanx: African American Soldiers in the War of Independence, the War of 1812, and the Civil War* (1887; reprint, New York: Da Capo Press, 1994), 200; Thomas D. Morris, *Southern Slavery and the Law, 1619–1860* (Chapel Hill: University of North Carolina Press, 1996), 266–71; Richard Slotkin, *No Quarter: The Battle of the Crater, 1864* (New York: Random House, 2009), 108; Cornish, *The Sable Arm*, 158, 159.

10. Mark A. Lause, *Race and Radicalism in the Union Army* (Urbana: University of Illinois Press, 2009), 93, 101.

11. General Orders No. 60, August 21, 1862, in U.S. War Department, *The War of the Rebellion: A Compilation of the Official Records of the Union and Confederate Armies*, 128 vols. (Washington, DC: Government Printing Office, 1880–1901), ser. 1, vol. 14, p. 599 (hereafter *OR*); H. W. Mercer to [Thomas] Jordan, November 14, 1862, and endorsement by James A. Seddon, n.d., *OR*, ser. 2, vol. 4, pp. 945–46.

12. General Orders No. 111, A Proclamation by the President of the Confederate States, December 24, 1862, *OR*, ser. 2, vol. 5, pp. 796–97; Jefferson Davis to the Senate and House of Representatives of the Confederate States, January 12, 1863, *OR*, ser. 2, vol. 5, pp. 807–8; George R. Browder, February 7, 1863, in Richard L. Troutman, ed., *The Heavens Are Weeping: The Diaries of George R. Browder, 1852–1886* (Grand Rapids, MI: Zondervan Publishing, 1987), 146.

13. James A. Seddon to John C. Pemberton, April 8, 1863, *OR*, ser. 2, vol. 5, p. 867; Joint resolutions adopted by the Confederate Congress on the subject of retaliation April 30–May 1, 1863, May 1, 1863, *OR*, 940–41.

14. Kirby Smith to Samuel Cooper and enclosures, June 16, 1863, H. L. Clay to Kirby Smith, July 13, 1863, *OR*, ser. 2, vol. 6, pp. 21, 22, 115.

15. John Fabian Witt, *Lincoln's Code: The Laws of War in American History* (New York: Free Press, 2012), 249.

16. General Orders No. 100, April 24, 1863, Instructions for the Government of Armies of the United States in the Field, *OR*, ser. 3, vol. 3, pp. 153, 155; George S. Burkhardt, *Confederate Rage, Yankee Wrath: No Quarter in the Civil War* (Carbondale: Southern Illinois University Press, 2007), 78.

17. Charles Sumner to Lincoln, May 20, 1863, Abraham Lincoln Papers, Manuscript Division, Library of Congress (hereafter LPLC).

18. Theodore Hodgkins to E. M. Stanton, April 18, 1864, in Berlin, ed., *The Black Military Experience*, 587.

19. Cornish, *The Sable Arm*, 163–68; Noah Andre Trudeau, *Like Men of War: Black Troops in the Civil War, 1862–1865* (Boston: Little, Brown, 1998), 97–102; Cornish, *The Sable Arm*, 172, 180; Nathan W. Daniels, March 14, 1863, in C. P. Weaver, ed., *Thank God My Regiment an African One: The Civil War Diary of Colonel Nathan W. Daniels* (Baton Rouge: Louisiana State University Press, 1998), 54; James G. Hollandsworth Jr., "The Execution of White Officers from Black Units by Confederate Forces during the Civil War," *Louisiana History* 35 (Fall 1994): 477, 483, 485, 489 (Table 3); William C. Davis, *Lincoln's Men: How President Lincoln Became Father to an Army and a Nation* (New York: Free Press, 1999), 161.

20. Douglass to George L. Stearns, August 1, 1863, and Douglass, "The Commander-in-Chief and His Black Soldiers" (August 1863), *Douglass' Monthly*, in Philip S. Foner, ed., *The Life and Writings of Frederick Douglass*, 5 vols. (New York: International Publishers, 1952–75), 3:369–70.

21. Lincoln, Order of Retaliation, July 30, 1863, 6:357; General Orders No. 252, July 31, 1863, *OR*, ser. 2, vol. 6, p. 163; Henry Louis Gates Jr., *Lincoln on Race and Slavery* (Princeton: Princeton University Press, 2009), 276.

22. Cornish, *The Sable Arm*, 171–79; Trudeau, *Like Men of War*, 167–68, 193–94, 245–47, 274; Lincoln, Address at Sanitary Fair, Baltimore, Maryland, April 18, 1864, *CW*, 7:302.

23. Robert Knox Sneden, May 3–8, 1864, in Charles E. Bryan Jr. and Nelson D. Lankford, eds., *Eye of the Storm: A Civil War Odyssey* (New York: Free Press, 2000), 225.

24. Glatthaar, *Forged in Battle*, 172.

25. Cornish, *The Sable Arm*, 183–87; James M. McPherson, *The Struggle for Equality: Abolitionists and the Negro in the Civil War and Reconstruction* (1964; reprint, Princeton: Princeton University Press, 1995), 212–13; General Orders No. 163, June 4, 1863, *OR*, ser. 3, vol. 3, p. 252; Luis F. Emilio, *A Brave Black Regiment: The History of the 54th Massachusetts,*

1863–1865 (1894; reprint, New York: Da Capo Press, 1995), 221; Wilbur Fisk to *Montpelier Green Mountain Freeman*, June 19, 1864, in Emil Rosenblatt and Ruth Rosenblatt, eds., *Hard Marching Every Day: The Civil War Letters of Private Wilbur Fisk, 1861–1865* (1983; reprint, Lawrence: University Press of Kansas, 1992), 231.

26. William Dusinberre, *Civil War Issues in Philadelphia, 1856–1865* (Philadelphia: University of Pennsylvania Press, 1965), 165n18.

27. Michael O. Smith, "Raising a Black Regiment in Michigan: Adversity and Triumph," *Michigan Historical Review* 16 (Fall 1990): 32.

28. David Tod to Edwin M. Stanton, June 27, 1863, with printed correspondence, LPLC.

29. Douglass, "Duty of Colored Men" (August 1863), *Douglass' Monthly*, in Foner, ed., *The Life and Writings of Frederick Douglass*, 3:373; James Henry Gooding in *New Bedford Mercury*, August 21, December 4, 1863, and Gooding to Lincoln, September 28, 1863, in Adams, ed., *On the Altar of Freedom*, 49, 83, 119–20.

30. Frederick Douglass, *Life and Times of Frederick Douglass Written by Himself. His Early Life as a Slave, His Escape from Bondage, and His Complete History* (1892; reprint, New York: Macmillan, 1962), 348.

31. "Frederick Douglass on President Lincoln," *Liberator*, September 16, 1864, p. 151; Jim Downs, *Sick from Freedom: African-American Illness and Suffering during the Civil War and Reconstruction* (New York: Oxford University Press, 2012), 26.

32. Sergt. John F. Shorter et al. to Lincoln, July 16, 1864, in Berlin, ed., *The Black Military Experience*, 401.

33. McPherson, *Struggle for Equality*, 214, 215, 217; Thomas Wentworth Higginson, "Appendix D—The Struggle for Pay," in *Army Life in a Black Regiment* (1869; reprint, Boston: Beacon Press, 1962), 280–81. A transcription of Walker's court-martial appears in Mark M. Smith, ed., *Slavery in North America: From the Colonial Period to Emancipation*, 4 vols. (London: Pickering and Chatto, 2009), 4:237–64.

34. Christian G. Samito, *Becoming American under Fire: Irish Americans, African Americans, and the Politics of Citizenship during the Civil War Era* (Ithaca: Cornell University Press, 2009), 96.

35. Edwin M. Stanton, Report of the Secretary of War, December 5, 1863, in *Message of the President of the United States, and Accompanying Documents, to the Two Houses of Congress, at the Commencement of the First Session of the Thirty-Eighth Congress* (Washington, DC: Government Printing Office, 1863), 8; Thomas Wentworth Higginson to the editor, *New York Tribune*, January 22, 1864, in Higginson, *Army Life in a Black Regiment*, 284; Edward Bates to Lincoln, April 23, 1864, *OR*, ser. 3, vol. 4, pp. 273–74.

36. George Washington to Lincoln, December 4, 1864, in Ira Berlin et al., eds., *Freedom: A Documentary History of Emancipation, 1861–1867*. Ser. I, vol. I. *The Destruction of Slavery* (Cambridge: Cambridge University Press, 1985), 608; Keith P. Wilson, *Campfires of Freedom: The Camp Life of Black Soldiers during the Civil War* (Kent: Kent State University Press, 2002), 47, 181.

37. Richard D. Sears, *"A Practical Recognition of the Brotherhood of Man": John G. Fee and the Camp Nelson Experience* (Berea, KY: Berea College Press, 1986), 3.

38. Joseph Smith to Mr. President, January 10, 1865, in Ira Berlin et al., eds., *Freedom: A Documentary History of Emancipation, 1861–1867*. Ser. I, vol. 2. *The Wartime Genesis of Free Labor: The Upper South* (Cambridge: Cambridge University Press, 1993), 693–94.

39. McPherson, *Struggle for Equality*, 213–14, 217; General Orders No. 215, June 22, 1864, *OR*, ser. 3, vol. 4, p. 448.

40. Thomas Wentworth Higginson to the editor, *New York Tribune*, August 12, 1864, in Higginson, *Army Life in a Black Regiment*, 289; General Orders No. 31, March 8, 1865, *OR*, ser. 3, vol. 4, p. 1223; Cornish, *The Sable Arm*, 194–95; B. W. Brice, "Bounties to Colored Troops," May 26, 1865, *OR*, ser. 3, vol. 5, pp. 659–60; Eric Foner, *The Fiery Trial: Abraham Lincoln and American Slavery* (New York: W. W. Norton, 2010), 254; Berlin, ed., *The Black Military Experience*, 766n.

4. Battles, Massacres, Parades

1. William Todd, *The Seventy-Ninth Highlanders: New York Volunteers in the War of Rebellion, 1861–1865* (Albany: Press of Brandow, Barton, 1886), 170.

2. Chandra Manning, *What This Cruel War Was Over: Soldiers, Slavery, and the Civil War* (New York: Alfred A. Knopf, 2007), 12, 13, 83, 95–96.

3. David M. Gold, "Frustrated Glory: John Frances Appleton and Black Soldiers in the Civil War," *Maine Historical Society Quarterly* 31 (Summer 1991): 182–83.

4. Chandra Manning, "Wartime Nationalism and Race," in William J. Cooper Jr. and John M. McCardell Jr., eds., *In the Cause of Liberty: How the Civil War Redefined American Ideals* (Baton Rouge: Louisiana State University Press, 2009), 102.

5. Dudley Taylor Cornish, "African American Troops in the Union Army," in Richard N. Current, ed., *Encyclopedia of the Confederacy*, 4 vols. (New York: Simon and Schuster, 1993), 1:12.

6. Charles Sumner, December 24, 1864, in Don E. Fehrenbacher and Virginia Fehrenbacher, eds., *Recollected Words of Abraham Lincoln* (Stanford: Stanford University Press, 1996), 435.

7. Lincoln to John A. Dix, January 14, 1863, in Roy P. Basler, ed., *Collected Works of Abraham Lincoln*, 8 vols. (New Brunswick: Rutgers University Press, 1953), 6:56 (hereafter *CW*).

8. Lincoln to Andrew Johnson, September 18, 1863, *CW*, 6:462.

9. William T. Sherman to Edwin M. Stanton, October 25, 1864, in Brooks D. Simpson and Jean V. Berlin, eds., *Sherman's Civil War: Selected Correspondence of William T. Sherman, 1860–1865* (Chapel Hill: University of North Carolina Press, 1999), 741.

10. William A. Dobak, *Freedom by the Sword: The U.S. Colored Troops, 1862–1867* (Washington, DC: Center of Military History, U.S. Army, 2011), 499, 498.

11. Noah Andre Trudeau, *Like Men of War: Black Troops in the Civil War, 1862–1865* (Boston: Little, Brown, 1998), xix; Dudley Taylor Cornish, *The Sable Arm: Negro Troops in the Union Army, 1861–1865* (1956; reprint, New York: W. W. Norton, 1966), 265; Edwin M. Stanton, Report of the Secretary of War, December 5, 1863, in *Message of the President of the United States, and Accompanying Documents, to the Two Houses of Congress, at the Commencement of the First Session of the Thirty-Eighth Congress* (Washington, DC: Government Printing Office, 1863), 8.

12. Bell Irvin Wiley, *Southern Negroes, 1861–1865* (1938; reprint, New Haven: Yale University Press, 1965), 334, 336, 340; Bell Irvin Wiley, *The Life of Billy Yank: The Common Soldier of the Union* (1952; reprint, Indianapolis: Bobbs-Merrill, 1962), 314.

13. Mark A. Lause, *Race and Radicalism in the Union Army* (Urbana: University of Illinois Press, 2009), 70–71, 5.

14. Trudeau, *Like Men of War*, 467.

15. Ibid., 44–45; William H. Leckie and Shirley A. Leckie, *Unlikely Warriors: General Benjamin Grierson and His Family* (Norman: University of Oklahoma Press, 1984), 101; Joseph J. Scroggs Diary, September 29, 1864, 20, U.S. Military History Institute, Carlisle Barracks, PA.

16. Trudeau, *Like Men of War*, 46–58; Joseph A. Glatthaar, *Forged in Battle: The Civil War Alliance of Black Soldiers and White Officers* (New York: Free Press, 1990), 134; Charles A. Dana, *Recollections of the Civil War* (1898; reprint, New York: Collier Books, 1963), 93.

17. Cornish, *The Sable Arm*, 265; correspondence, February 26, 1864, in *Liberator*, March 18, 1864, in Virginia M. Adams, ed., *On the Altar of Freedom: A Black Soldier's Civil War Letters from the Front* (Amherst: University of Massachusetts Press, 1991), 115; Donald Yacovone, ed., *A Voice of Thunder: The Civil War Letters of George E. Stephens* (Urbana: University of Illinois Press, 1997), 67; Trudeau, *Like Men of War*, 138, 152; William H. Nulty, *Confederate Florida: The Road to Olustee* (Tuscaloosa: University of Alabama Press, 1990), 203, 209, 211; J. Matthew

Gallman, "In Your Hands That Musket Means Liberty: African American Soldiers and the Battle of Olustee," in Joan Waugh and Gary W. Gallagher, eds., *Wars within a War: Controversy and Conflict over the American Civil War* (Chapel Hill: University of North Carolina Press, 2009), 105.

18. John Cimprich, *Fort Pillow, a Civil War Massacre and Public Memory* (Baton Rouge: Louisiana State University Press, 2005), 80; Mark E. Neely Jr., *Retaliation: The Problem of Atrocity in the American Civil War* (Gettysburg: Gettysburg College, 2002), 24.

19. Lincoln, Address at Sanitary Fair, Baltimore, Maryland, April 18, 1864, *CW*, 7:302–3.

20. Cimprich, *Fort Pillow*, 99–101.

21. Lincoln to Cabinet Members, May 3, 1863, *CW*, 7:328; Edward Bates to Lincoln, May 4, 1864, Abraham Lincoln Papers, Manuscript Division, Library of Congress (hereafter LPLC); Edward Bates, May 9, 1864, in Howard K. Beale, ed., *The Diary of Edward Bates, 1859–1866* (Washington, DC: Government Printing Office, 1933), 365.

22. Gideon Welles to Lincoln, May 5, 1864, LPLC; Gideon Welles, May 3, 1864, in Howard K. Beale, ed., *Diary of Gideon Welles: Secretary of the Navy Under Lincoln and Johnson*, 2 vols. (New York: W. W. Norton, 1960), 2:24; John P. Usher to Lincoln, May 6, 1864, LPLC.

23. Montgomery Blair to Lincoln, May 6, 1864, William M. Stanton to Lincoln, May 5, 1864, Salmon P. Chase to Lincoln, May 6, 1864, LPLC.

24. Lincoln to Edwin M. Stanton, May 17, 1864, *CW*, 7:345–46; Cimprich, *Fort Pillow*, 101–2; Paul D. Escott, *"What Shall We Do with the Negro?" Lincoln, White Racism, and Civil War America* (Charlottesville: University of Virginia Press, 2009), 99.

25. Lincoln to Stanton, May 17, 1864, *CW*, 7:345–46.

26. Andrew Ward, *River Run Red: The Fort Pillow Massacre in the American Civil War* (New York: Viking, 2005), 325; Michael Burlingame, *Lincoln and the Civil War* (Carbondale: Southern Illinois University Press, 2011), 108; Gregory J. W. Urwin, "Sowing the Wind and Reaping the Whirlwind: Abraham Lincoln as a War President," in Randall M. Miller, ed., *Lincoln and Leadership: Military, Political, and Religious Decision Making* (New York: Fordham University Press, 2012), 57–58.

27. Lincoln to Charles Sumner, May 19, 1864, in Roy P. Basler, ed., *The Collected Works of Abraham Lincoln, Supplement, 1832–1865* (Westport: Greenwood Press, 1974), 243.

28. Roy P. Basler, "And for His Widow and His Orphan," *Quarterly Journal of the Library of Congress* 27 (October 1970): 291–94.

29. Trudeau, *Like Men of War*, 220–28; Benjamin Quarles, *The Negro in the Civil War* (1953; reprint, Boston: Little, Brown, 1969), 299; Charles

Torrey Beman to unidentified newspaper, June 20, 1864, in Edwin S. Redkey, ed., *A Grand Army of Black Men: Letters from African-American Soldiers in the Union Army, 1861–1865* (Cambridge: Cambridge University Press, 1992), 99; Trudeau, *Like Men of War*, 226.

30. Ulysses S. Grant to Daniel Ammen, August 18, 1864, in John Y. Simon, ed., *The Papers of Ulysses S. Grant*, 32 vols. (Carbondale: Southern Illinois University Press, 1967–2012), 12:35.

31. Edward Bates, August 2, 1864, in Beale, ed., *The Diary of Edward Bates*, 393.

32. James M. McPherson, *Battle Cry of Freedom: The Civil War Era* (New York: Oxford University Press, 1988), 740; Wilbur Fisk to *Montpelier Green Mountain Freeman*, June 19, 1864, in Emil Rosenblatt and Ruth Rosenblatt, eds., *Hard Marching Every Day: The Civil War Letters of Private Wilbur Fisk, 1861–1865* (1983; reprint, Lawrence: University Press of Kansas, 1992), 230.

33. "Letter from Chaplain Hunter," *Christian Recorder* 4, no. 29 (July 16, 1864): 114.

34. Trudeau, *Like Men of War*, 229–234; William Marvel, *Burnside* (Chapel Hill: University of North Carolina Press, 1991), 393; Michael A. Cavanaugh and William Marvel, *The Petersburg Campaign, The Battle of the Crater, "The Horrid Pit," June 25–August 6, 1864* (Lynchburg, VA: H. E. Howard, 1989), 18; McPherson, *Battle Cry of Freedom*, 758.

35. Trudeau, *Like Men of War*, 234–235; Marvel, *Burnside*, 399.

36. William H. Thomas to Theodore D. Jervey, July 30, 1911, Theodore D. Jervey Papers, South Carolina Historical Society.

37. Michael E. Stevens, ed., *As If It Were Glory: Robert Beecham's Civil War from the Iron Brigade to the Black Regiments* (Madison: Madison House, 1998), 183, 184; Trudeau, *Like Men of War*, 236–43.

38. Marvel, *Burnside*, 404; Edward A. Miller Jr., *The Black Civil War Soldiers of Illinois* (Columbia: University of South Carolina Press, 1998), 74; Quarles, *The Negro in the Civil War*, 304; Trudeau, *Like Men of War*, 244, 246; Gary W. Gallagher, ed., *Fighting for the Confederacy: The Personal Recollections of General Edward Porter Alexander* (Chapel Hill: University of North Carolina Press, 1989), 462.

39. Bryce A. Suderow, "The Battle of the Crater: The Civil War's Worst Massacre," *Civil War History* 43 (September 1997): 219–24; Trudeau, *Like Men of War*, 247; Cavanaugh and Marvel, *The Petersburg Campaign*, 128; Cornish, *The Sable Arm*, 276; Glatthaar, *Forged in Battle*, 150; Ulysses S. Grant to Henry W. Halleck, August 1, 1864, in Simon, ed., *The Papers of Ulysses S. Grant*, 11:361.

40. Orlando B. Willcox to Eb[en] N. Willcox, August 3, 1864, William V. Richards to Marie Willcox, August 6, 1864, in Robert Garth Scott, ed., *Forgotten Valor: The Memoirs, Journals, and Civil War Letters of*

Orlando B. Willcox (Kent: Kent State University Press, 1999), 557, 560; George F. Cram to mother, August 9, 1864, in Jennifer Cain Bohrnstedt, ed., *Soldiering with Sherman: The Civil War Letters of George F. Cram* (DeKalb: Northern Illinois University Press, 2000), 133.

41. Ambrose E. Burnside testimony, August 12, 1864, in U.S. War Department, *The War of the Rebellion: A Compilation of the Official Records of the Union and Confederate Armies*, 128 vols. (Washington, DC: Government Printing Office, 1880–1901), ser. 1, vol. 40, pt. 1, p. 73 (hereafter *OR*); Bruce Tap, *Over Lincoln's Shoulder: The Committee on the Conduct of the War* (Lawrence: University Press of Kansas, 1998), 191; Cornish, *The Sable Arm*, 274.

42. Cornish, *The Sable Arm*, 310.

43. Frederick S. Eaton, "Colored Troops," *American Missionary* 8 (November 1864): 274.

44. Trudeau, *Like Men of War*, 284–94; Glatthaar, *Forged in Battle*, 151; Thomas Morris Chester, "Headquarters, Chapin's Farm," October 17, 1864, in *Philadelphia Press*, in R. J. M. Blackett, ed., *Thomas Morris Chester: Black Civil War Correspondent, His Dispatches from the Virginia Front* (Baton Rouge: Louisiana State University Press, 1989), 150, 153.

45. Lincoln, Annual Message to Congress, December 8, 1863, *CW*, 7:50.

46. Lincoln to Albert G. Hodges, April 4, 1864, *CW*, 7:282.

47. Lincoln, Interview with Alexander W. Randall and Joseph T. Mills, August 19, 1864, *CW*, 7:506–7.

48. Lincoln to Isaac M. Schermerhorn [unfinished draft], September 12, 1864, *CW*, 8:1–2.

49. Richard Slotkin, *No Quarter: The Battle of the Crater, 1864* (New York: Random House, 2009), 335–36.

50. Benjamin Quarles, *Lincoln and the Negro* (New York: Oxford University Press, 1962), 233.

51. Trudeau, *Like Men of War*, 338–49; James B. Steedman, January 27, 1865, *OR*, ser. 1, vol. 45, pt. 1, p. 508.

52. Jane Welcome to Lincoln, November 21, 1864, Rosanna Henson to Lincoln, July 11, 1864, in Ira Berlin, ed., *Freedom: A Documentary History of Emancipation, 1861–1867.* Ser. 2. *The Black Military Experience* (Cambridge: Cambridge University Press, 1982), 664, 680 (emphasis in original).

53. Hannah Johnson to Lincoln, July 31, 1863, in Berlin, ed., *Black Military Experience*, 582.

54. Ibid., 582–83.

55. William C. Davis, *Lincoln's Men: How President Lincoln Became Father to an Army and a Nation* (New York: Free Press, 1999), 164.

56. Trudeau, *Like Men of War*, 206–208; Slotkin, *No Quarter*, 91.

57. Horace Porter, *Campaigning with Grant* (New York: Century, 1897), 217–18; Sylvanus Cadwallader, *Three Years with Grant as Recalled by War Correspondent Sylvanus Cadwallader*, ed. Benjamin P. Thomas (1955; reprint, Lincoln: University of Nebraska Press, 1996), 232.

58. Porter, *Campaigning with Grant*, 219–20; Cadwallader, *Three Years with Grant*, 233; Slotkin, *No Quarter*, 22.

59. Thomas Morris Chester, "Army of the James," *Philadelphia Press*, March 21, 1865, in Blackett, ed., *Thomas Morris Chester*, 277; Fehrenbacher and Fehrenbacher, eds., *Recollected Words of Abraham Lincoln*, 168.

60. Trudeau, *Like Men of War*, 416; John C. Brock, "Death of the President," *Christian Recorder* 5, no. 18 (May 6, 1865): 69.

61. George Washington Williams, *A History of the Negro Troops in the War of the Rebellion, 1861–1865* (1887; reprint, New York: Fordham University Press, 2012), 210–11.

62. William O. Stoddard, "White House Sketches No. 7," in Michael Burlingame, ed., *Inside the White House in War Times: Memoirs and Reports of Lincoln's Secretary* (Lincoln: University of Nebraska Press, 2000), 172–73.

63. Brian R. Dirck, *Abraham Lincoln and White America* (Lawrence: University Press of Kansas, 2012), 133, 152–53.

64. Bell Irvin Wiley, *Kingdom Coming: The Emancipation Proclamation of September 22, 1862, An Address Delivered at the Chicago Historical Society, September 21, 1962* (Chicago: Chicago Historical Society, 1963), 17; Lincoln to Albert G. Hodges, April 4, 1864, *CW*, 7:282.

65. Benjamin Quarles, *Lincoln and the Negro*, 235; Trudeau, *Like Men of War*, 417–24.

66. Brock, "Death of the President"; Ervin L. Jordan Jr., "'Traitors Shall Not Dictate to Us': Afro-Virginians and the Unfinished Emancipation of 1865," in William C. Davis and James I. Robertson Jr., eds., *Virginia at War: 1865* (Lexington: University Press of Kentucky, 2012), 107; Garland H. White, "Letter from Richmond," in *Christian Recorder* 5, no. 16 (April 22, 1865): 62.

67. Thomas Morris Chester, "Hall of Congress," *Philadelphia Press*, April 6, 1865, in Blackett, ed., *Thomas Morris Chester*, 294, 295, 297.

Afterword

1. Benjamin Quarles, *Lincoln and the Negro* (New York: Oxford University Press, 1962), 241–42; Merrill D. Peterson, *Lincoln in American Memory* (New York: Oxford University Press, 1994), 14–15; Noah Andre Trudeau, *Like Men of War: Black Troops in the Civil War, 1862–1865* (Boston: Little, Brown, 1998), 433–34.

2. Quarles, *Lincoln and the Negro*, 242; William A. Dobak, *Freedom by the Sword: The U.S. Colored Troops, 1862–1867* (Washington, DC: Center of Military History, U.S. Army, 2011), 421.

3. Richard Slotkin, *No Quarter: The Battle of the Crater, 1864* (New York: Random House, 2009), 21.

4. Harriet Tubman in Rosa Belle Holt, "A Heroine in Ebony," *Chautauquan* 23 (July 1896): 462.

5. Bell Irvin Wiley, *Southern Negroes, 1861–1865* (1938; reprint, New Haven: Yale University Press, 1965), 15.

6. James C. Taylor, "From the Ninety-Third U.S.C.T.," April 14, 1865, *Christian Recorder* 5, no. 18 (May 6, 1865): 71; I. N. Triplett, "Convention of Iowa Colored Soldiers," *Muscatine (Iowa) Journal*, November 6, 1865, in *Christian Recorder* 5, no. 46 (November 18, 1865): 181.

7. J. G. Randall and Richard N. Current, *Lincoln the President: Last Full Measure* (New York: Dodd, Mead, 1955), 320–21; Michael Burlingame, *Abraham Lincoln: A Life*, 2 vols. (Baltimore: Johns Hopkins University Press, 2008), 2:750.

8. Robert Dale Owen, James McKaye, and Samuel G. G. Howe, to Edwin M. Stanton, June 30, 1863, in U.S. War Department, *The War of the Rebellion: A Compilation of the Official Records of the Union and Confederate Armies*, 128 vols. (Washington, DC: Government Printing Office, 1880–1901), ser. 3, vol. 3, p. 436.

9. James T. Ayers, April 20, 1864, in John Hope Franklin, ed., *Civil War Diary of James T. Ayers* (Springfield: Illinois State Historical Society, 1947), 5.

10. Christopher C. Andrews to Lincoln, November 3, 1864, Abraham Lincoln Papers, Manuscript Division, Library of Congress (hereafter LPLC); Peterson, *Lincoln in American Memory*, 56; William Murrell in Barbara Gannon, *The Won Cause: Black and White Comradeship in the Grand Army of the Republic* (Chapel Hill: University of North Carolina Press, 2011), 70–71.

11. B. A. Botkin, *Lay My Burden Down: A Folk History of Slavery* (1945; reprint, Athens: University of Georgia Press, 1989), 240, 16.

12. John Barr, "African American Memory and the Great Emancipator," in Robert P. Watson, William D. Pederson, and Frank J. Williams, eds., *Lincoln's Enduring Legacy: Perspectives from Great Thinkers, Great Leaders, and the American Experiment* (Lanham: Lexington Books, 2011), 159.

13. Barry Schwartz, *Abraham Lincoln in the Post-Heroic Era: History and Memory in Late Twentieth-Century America* (Chicago: University of Chicago Press, 2008), 139; Jackie Hogan, *Lincoln, Inc.: Selling the Sixteenth President in Contemporary America* (Lanham, MD: Rowman and Littlefield, 2011), 127, 183n42.

14. Benjamin Quarles, *The Negro in the Civil War* (1953; reprint, Boston: Little, Brown, 1969), 345; Joseph A. Glatthaar, *Forged in Battle: The Civil War Alliance of Black Soldiers and White Officers* (New York: Free Press, 1990), 209.

15. Gus to Lydia, December 12, 1863, George L. Gaskill to sister, April 23, 1865, in Glatthaar, *Forged in Battle*, 208–9; James Madison Bowler to Lizzie, April [18?], 1865, in Andrea R. Foroughi, ed., *Go If You Think It Your Duty: A Minnesota Couple's Civil War Letters* (St. Paul: Minnesota Historical Society Press, 2008), 290.

16. Trudeau, *Like Men of War*, 433.

17. Anderson Ruffin Abbott, "Some Recollections of Lincoln's Assassination," *Anglo-American Magazine* [London] 5, no. 5 (May 1901): 401.

18. Glatthaar, *Forged in Battle*, 209; Chauncey Leonard to Lorenzo Thomas, April 30, 1865, in Ira Berlin, ed., *Freedom: A Documentary History of Emancipation, 1861–1867*. Ser. 2. *The Black Military Experience* (Cambridge: Cambridge University Press, 1982), 652.

19. Edgar Dinsmore to Carrie Drayton, May 29, 1865, Edgar Dinsmore Papers, 1864–1865, David M. Rubenstein Rare Book and Manuscript Library, Duke University.

20. Allen C. Guelzo, "How Abe Lincoln Lost the Black Vote: Lincoln and Emancipation in the African American Mind," *Journal of the Abraham Lincoln Association* 25 (Winter 2004): 5–6.

21. Elijah P. Marrs, *Life and History of the Rev. Elijah P. Marrs, First Pastor of Beargrass Baptist Church, and Author* (1885; reprint, Miami: Mnemosyne Publishing, 1969), 18, 21, 23, 69.

22. Frank [Frances] A. Rollin, *Life and Public Services of Martin R. Delany, Sub-assistant Commissioner Bureau Relief of Refugees, Freedmen, and of Abandoned Lands, and Late Major 104th U.S. Colored Troops* (Boston: Lee and Shepard, 1883), 9–10, 166–71, 174, 177–80.

23. John Ernest, *A Nation within a Nation: Organizing African-American Communities before the Civil War* (Chicago: Ivan R. Dee, 2011), 105.

24. "The Colored Citizens of Xenia, Their prowess and Their Patriotism, Major Delany—A Negro 'in Full Uniform,' His Speech," *Xenia (Ohio) Sentinel*, March 17, 1865, in Robert S. Levine, ed., *Martin R. Delany: A Documentary Reader* (Chapel Hill: University of North Carolina Press, 2003), 389–91.

25. Martin R. Delany, "Monument to President Lincoln," *Christian Recorder* 5, no. 20 (May 20, 1865): 78; Martin R. Delany in *New York Weekly Anglo-African*, June 10, 1865, in Rollin, *Life and Public Services of Martin R. Delany*, 207; Delany, "Monument to President Lincoln."

26. Eric Ledell Smith, ed., "The Civil War Letters of Quartermaster Sergeant John C. Brock, 43rd Regiment, United States Colored Troops,"

in William Blair and William Pencak, eds., *Making and Remaking Pennsylvania's Civil War* (University Park: Pennsylvania State University Press, 2001), 141–64.

27. John C. Brock, "Death of the President," *Christian Recorder* 5, no. 18 (May 6, 1865): 69.

28. Ibid.

29. "Africano," in *New York Weekly Anglo African*, September 24, 1864, in Edwin S. Redkey, ed., *A Grand Army of Black Men* (Cambridge: Cambridge University Press, 1992), 212–13; Chandra Manning, *What This Cruel War Was Over: Soldiers, Slavery, and the Civil War* (New York: Alfred A. Knopf, 2007), 185.

30. William Hannibal Thomas, *The American Negro: What He Was, What He Is, and What He May Become: A Critical and Practical Discussion* (New York: MacMillan, 1901), xxi.

31. Richard Carwardine, *Lincoln: A Life of Purpose and Power* (New York: Vintage Books, 2007), 220–21.

32. Lincoln to Charles D. Robinson, August 17, 1864, in Roy P. Basler, ed., *Collected Works of Abraham Lincoln*, 8 vols. (New Brunswick: Rutgers University Press, 1953), 7:500 (hereafter *CW*).

33. Harold Holzer, *Emancipating Lincoln: The Proclamation in Text, Context, and Memory* (Cambridge: Harvard University Press, 2012), 152–53, 161.

34. Richard Slotkin, *The Long Road to Antietam: How the Civil War Became a Revolution* (New York: W. W. Norton, 2012), 411, 410; W. E. B. Du Bois, *Black Reconstruction: An Essay towards a History of the Part Which Black Folk Played in the Attempt to Reconstruct Democracy in America, 1860–1880* (Philadelphia: Saifer, 1935); Stephanie McCurry, *Confederate Reckoning: Power and Politics in the Civil War South* (Cambridge: Harvard University Press, 2010), 258–60, 262, 319.

35. Michael Vorenberg, *Final Freedom: The Civil War, the Abolition of Slavery, and the Thirteenth Amendment* (Cambridge: Cambridge University Press, 2001), 37.

36. Slotkin, *The Long Road to Antietam*, 410, 412; J. Matthew Gallman, "Snapshots: Images of Men in the United States Colored Troops," *American Nineteenth Century History* 12, no. 2 (2012): 130.

37. Bethuel Hunter, *"No Man Can Hinder Me": Black Troops in the Union Armies during the American Civil War* (New Haven: Beinecke Rare Book and Manuscript Library, 2003), 44.

38. Henry J. Maxwell, August 7, 1865, in Philip S. Foner and George E. Walker, eds., *Proceedings of the Black National and State Conventions, 1865–1900* (Philadelphia: Temple University Press, 1986), 116.

39. John Edward Bruce, "The 6th U.S.C. Troops," *Cleveland Gazette* 4, no. 30 (March 12, 1887): 1; Louis Willis, "An Old Soldier Talks," *Cleveland*

Gazette 4, no. 34 (April 9, 1887): 3; Burt G. Wilder, "Two Examples of the Negro's Courage, Physical and Moral," *Alexander's Magazine* 1, nos. 8–10 (January 1906): 24.

40. Melvin Claxton and Mark Puls, *Uncommon Valor: A Story of Race, Patriotism, and Glory in the Final Battles of the Civil War* (Hoboken: John Wiley and Sons, 2006), 214.

41. Dobak, *Freedom by the Sword*, 108, 499.

42. David Henson Slay, "New Masters on the Mississippi: The United States Colored Troops of the Middle Mississippi Valley" (Ph.D. diss., Texas Christian University, 2009), 207–8.

43. George Mike Arnold, "Colored Soldiers in the Union Army," *A.M.E. Church Review* 3 (October 1886): 258.

44. William K. Klingaman, *Abraham Lincoln and the Road to Emancipation, 1861–1865* (New York: Viking, 2001), 288–90.

45. Allen C. Guelzo, *Lincoln's Emancipation Proclamation: The End of Slavery in America* (New York: Simon and Schuster, 2004), 218.

46. Lincoln, Response to a Serenade, February 1, 1865, *CW*, 8:254.

47. Gallman, "Snapshots: Images of Men in the United States Colored Troops," 130.

48. J. Matthew Gallman, "In Your Hands That Musket Means Liberty: African American Soldiers and the Battle of Olustee," in Joan Waugh and Gary W. Gallagher, eds., *Wars within a War: Controversy and Conflict over the American Civil War* (Chapel Hill: University of North Carolina Press, 2009), 96–97.

49. J. Matthew Gallman, *Mastering Wartime: A Social History of Philadelphia during the Civil War* (Cambridge: Cambridge University Press, 1990), 48n172; Donald R. Shaffer, *After the Glory: The Struggles of Black Civil War Veterans* (Lawrence: University Press of Kansas, 2004), chapter 3.

50. *Equal Suffrage. Address from the Colored Citizens of Norfolk, Va., to the People of the United States* (New Bedford, MA: E. Anthony and Sons, 1865), 2.

51. Eric Foner, *The Fiery Trial: Abraham Lincoln and American Slavery* (New York: W. W. Norton, 2010), 283.

52. Manning, *What This Cruel War Was Over*, 3, 129, 130; Quarles, *The Negro in the Civil War*, 199.

53. Foner, *The Fiery Trial*, 244, 255–56.

54. Interview with Andrew Evans, 1932, *St. Louis Globe-Democrat*, July 31, 1932, in John W. Blassingame, ed., *Slave Testimony: Two Centuries of Letters, Speeches, Interviews and Autobiographies* (Baton Rouge: Louisiana State University Press, 1977), 586.

55. Stephen B. Oates, *Builders of the Dream: Abraham Lincoln and Martin Luther King Jr.* (Fort Wayne: Louis A. Warren Lincoln Library and Museum, 1982), 8.

INDEX

John David Smith is the Charles H. Stone Distinguished Professor of American History at the University of North Carolina at Charlotte. His publications include *A Just and Lasting Peace: A Documentary History of Reconstruction*; *Black Voices from Reconstruction, 1865–1877*; *Black Judas: William Hannibal Thomas and "The American Negro"*; *An Old Creed for the New South: Proslavery Ideology and Historiography, 1865–1918*; and (with Patricia Bellis Bixel) *Seeing the New South: Race and Place in the Photographs of Ulrich Bonnell Phillips*.

This series of concise books fills a need for short studies of the life, times, and legacy of President Abraham Lincoln. Each book gives readers the opportunity to quickly achieve basic knowledge of a Lincoln-related topic. These books bring fresh perspectives to well-known topics, investigate previously overlooked subjects, and explore in greater depth topics that have not yet received book-length treatment. For a complete list of current and forthcoming titles, see www.conciselincolnlibrary.com.

Other Books in the Concise Lincoln Library

*Abraham Lincoln and
Horace Greeley*
Gregory A. Borchard

Lincoln and the Civil War
Michael Burlingame

Lincoln and the Constitution
Brian R. Dirck

Lincoln and the Election of 1860
Michael S. Green

Lincoln and the Union Governors
William C. Harris

Lincoln and Reconstruction
John C. Rodrigue

Lincoln and Medicine
Glenna R. Schroeder-Lein

Lincoln and Race
Richard Striner

Lincoln as Hero
Frank J. Williams

*Abraham and
Mary Lincoln*
Kenneth J. Winkle